A Forehead Like Flint

How to blast through your brick walls
and come out smiling!

John Dunn

Published by:
Perissos Media
www.PerissosMedia.com

ISBN-13: 978-1723440519

CONTENTS

FOREWORD.. 5

CHAPTER 1 ~ GROWING UP 6

New Toys.. 9

Vision of Eternity 11

A New Love 14

CHAPTER 2 ~ THE WORLD NEEDS TO KNOW!........................ 17

Joseph's Early Arrival 18

Farmer Evangelist.. 21

He Is Alive... 27

CHAPTER 3 ~ LEARNING TO WALK 30

Dreams of Christ.. 31

Bible Study-Living Waters 34

CHAPTER 4 ~ THIS MEANS WAR! 40

Escape Artist.. 43

Confrontation... 46

CHAPTER 5 ~ HAVE BAGS, WILL TRAVEL! 50

Everything 61

CHAPTER 6 ~ STREET PREACHER 65

Monument of Judgement... 67

A Bold Challenge 70

Doubting Sister.. 72

Living by Faith 76

A Sign to Swindon... 78

Highs and Lows... 82

A Wee Scot Named Tom.. 85

Angry Paul... 88

Troubled Tyler... 89

Peter the Puncher 91

Reaching the Muslims 93

Heartbreaking News 97

CHAPTER 7 ~ ISRAEL AND PAKISTAN 99

The Battle of the Passport 101

Reality Bites 105

Continuing On 110

Walking Boots 112

Back to the Holy Land.. 116

Pakistan Revisited 121

Jarranwala... 123

Sahiwal 126

Great… 130

CHAPTER 8 ~ A BAD CASE OF LARYNGITIS 134

From Bad to Worse 137

Then I Awoke... 138

A New Beginning.. 142

EPILOGUE 147

A FINAL WORD TO THE READER 150

FOREWORD

My primary purpose for writing this book is to be obedient to my Lord, who has put it into my heart to endeavour to write an account of my life that will both, hopefully, inspire and encourage the reader to seek the Lord whilst He may be found.

Taking into consideration people's privacy, and out of respect, I will not always use peoples' real names, except for those of my family and where I deem it appropriate but, like John Bunyan in "The Pilgrim's Progress", I will use names that describe a certain characteristic or attribute of that particular person.

I will put forth an accurate account of the details of my life, as best as my memory serves me. I hope that, in the course of writing this book, there is no embarrassment brought to any person, and I hope that members of my family will not be hurt or offended by anything that is shared in these pages, for that is not the purpose of this book. I'm sure that there will be things that some people will disagree with, or things that they may find offensive or hard to believe- all that is shared in these pages is truth, I was there, I saw these things, they are all personal experiences.

When writing an autobiography there is always a debate with oneself of what to include and what to leave out. Do I write an Encyclopedia Britannica or a short booklet? I have tried to write this book with minimal planning, allowing the Holy Spirit to guide me into what to write and what to leave out. I'm not an author or writer to any stretch of the imagination, so if the grammar is a bit raw, I apologise ahead of time.

Also, this book is not written to glorify John Dunn in any way. The things that I have done and the things that I have experienced have been by the grace of God alone, and all the glory and praise goes to Him and Him only, for that is the reason for writing this book.

So, to those who read this book, who already know the Lord, I pray that it will be a blessing to you and inspire you to greater things in the Lord. For those who read this book and do not know the Lord, I pray that this book will encourage you to take that step closer to the Lord and to enter into a life changing relationship with the Creator of the universe.

In His service, John Dunn

CHAPTER 1 ~ GROWING UP

" ...For the imagination of man's heart is evil from his youth..." - Genesis 8:21b

Now, I've met some people in my life that seem to have an amazing memory of their childhood. They are able to name all of their friends from school and recount, in minute detail, past events of their lives- I'm not one of those people...

I was born on the 3rd of April, 1967 to Alfred Ernest and Shirley Rosena Dunn. Due to complications in my mother's pregnancy, she was given a Police escort to Battle hospital, Reading, in Berkshire. On the Easter Monday of that year, I was born.

My earliest memory of school was being a flower in the school play, and dancing around the assembly hall to the sound of Vivaldi's " Four Seasons". Francis Bailey was the name of the first primary school that I attended with my two sisters, Jill and Linda, and my two brothers, Tony and Mark. Yes, I am the youngest of five children, and anyone who is the youngest child will know that you always remain the baby of the family in your mother's eyes...

I was blessed to have wonderful parents. My father went by the name of John, (even though that wasn't his real name. He was known by a few different names....) My mother was very house proud, everything was kept clean and tidy, and she worked constantly to keep it that way which sometimes was a losing battle with four men living in the house! My mother was always there for us, and mealtimes were never late. She had a real hard time raising us due to the absence of my father when he was kept at our Majesty's pleasure...She never complained.

My father was a carpenter by trade, and an extremely hard- working man. He was a better carpenter than he was a thief. Coming from the East End of London, and due to some very hard and sad circumstances in his family life, my father grew up rebelling against authority, which will always lead to a life of crime, and that was the life that my father chose. He had many claims to "fame" and as a boy, I would be thoroughly entertained listening to his many stories. He was imprisoned in every prison on mainland England, and on the Isle of Wight. He was on the cleaning party to clean the gallows for the last man to be hanged in England.

He shared a prison cell with Jack-the-hat McVitee, a criminal that the notorious Kray Twins shot dead in the Blind Beggar pub, in the East End of London. He was in a cycle race in which the world record time was broken. But one of his most notable achievements was that he was an SAS soldier (Special Air Service, the British Army's Special Forces). He was the first man to pass the Selection Course for the Territorial SAS (21ST SAS), and then take the Selection Course for the regular SAS (22ND SAS) and to pass them first time, and all within a short space of time. He was mentioned, by name, in Sir Peter De Billiare's (the British Army's most decorated soldier) Autobiography. He was certainly no angel but he was a great father.

Due to the influence of my father's stories and the life that he led and the fact that I looked up to my father, I became a thief early on in life. I remember at the age of about six, going to the shops with my best friend, and taking a carrier bag with me, and just putting things into the bag, whatsoever I saw that I liked, into the bag it would go. Then one day, the manager of the shop came up to me and said" Go and do your shopping elsewhere, sonny!" which shocked me, because he obviously knew I had things in the bag from his shop, but he let me take them on the mutual understanding that I didn't come back. I never returned to that particular shop to steal again. There were many more shops to choose from.

I would steal anything. If it looked like something I would like to have or play with, I would steal it. Of course, it wasn't too long before I got into trouble with the police. I remember a policeman came to our house in Bourne Road, Thatcham, and parked his motorcycle outside our house, and left his goggles tied to the handle of his bike. As he talked to my parents about my stealing, I decided that I would sneak out of the house and go and see my best friend. Of course, I took the opportunity to steal the policeman's goggles from off of the handlebars of his bike as I made my way to my friends' house!

When I was about 8 years old, due to the economic situation in our country, my father started to work abroad. Germany and Holland were the main countries that he went to, working as a carpenter. He told us though, many years later, that he was also working as a mercenary in Angola at that time.

One of the first gifts that my father gave to me, on one of his home visits from abroad, was a large Bowie knife. Looking back, it was a strange gift to give to a nine-year old boy, but I loved it. I had never seen a knife like it. As a child, my father had given to each of us boys a penknife with a "pig sticker", but this was way beyond anything I'd had before. I believe that this was a starting point in my life with a fascination of knives and swords, which later on in my teens, I learnt how to use through the practise of Martial Arts.

Now Bourne Road, where I grew up, was on a council estate. As a child, no matter how hard or weird your life may have been, to you it's just "normal". It was "normal" for us to see our father fighting with the neighbours. It was "normal" for there to be trouble. Our house was petrol-bombed. There was a petition, raised by the neighbours to the Council, to evict us. One day our next-door neighbours would be our friends, then the next day, they would be our enemies. This was life.

Looking back, it was a rough and tough life, but it was just "life" to us. Please don't get me wrong, I'm not saying that life was bad, on the contrary, I loved every minute of my childhood. I had parents that loved me and protected me. I had brothers and sisters that were great fun to be around.

We would go out "scrumping" together (stealing the neighbour's apples). We would make a go-kart from bits of wood and old pram wheels that we would salvage from the local dump, a place where we spent many happy hours, with the rats, looking through the rubbish to see what we could find to play with. We went for long walks across the green meadows that were spotted with yellow buttercups, returning home late when the sky was an inky blue. We would make a rope swing in a tree on the river bank and spend many hours swinging and plunging into the river.

We would walk across the fields, to an American school to have stone fights with the American children who were taught there. In the winter, we would go to the frozen ponds and break up the ice and then lay it on the train tracks to see the trains crush it as they fled past! We would play in the hay barns. One of our favourite barns to play in was one where there was a bull that roamed about in the field. It was a short sprint to the hay barn from the fence, and it was an adrenaline rush to run across that open ground, with a bull chasing you! We would go to the local swimming pool, and climb through the fence without paying, and then steal bottles of soda from the barn on the way out.

Life was good, but life was lawless. I did whatever I pleased, stealing, vandalising peoples' gardens, playing football in the streets, which was a great grief to the neighbours, who usually ended up phoning the police. It became a Sunday tradition that the police would come to "The Square" (as we called the cul-de-sac where we lived, due to the fact that it was square in shape) because of the complaints by angry neighbours.

New Toys

One of the advantages of having a father that worked abroad was that Europe seemed to have more advanced toys than England did at that time. So, my father would come home with some very exciting things. On one occasion, he brought home a pair of walkie talkie radios. This was a great present that we soon put to not -so- good use!

One of our neighbours, who we imaginatively called "Greyhaired" because he had grey hair, had kept our football after it had gone over into his garden for the hundredth time, which we thought was a little unfair. So, one day, armed with our new toy, we planned a rescue mission! So, we waited until we saw Greyhaired leave his house. Then we sent Stephen, our next-door neighbour and friend, in to recover the captured ball. Stephen had one radio, and my brother Mark and I kept watch outside, with the other one. This is how the conversation went…

"Okay, I'm in the house, I am in the house…over!" came the crackling voice on our radio.

" I'm in the kitchen….I am in the kitchen…cannot find the ball….over!"

" I'm moving to the living room… I am moving to the living room, over!"

"Is it still all clear, over?" Stephen asked.

"Yes, it's all clear, no Greyhaired, continue on…over!" we replied.

"Okay, I'm looking around…cannot see the ball…cannot see the ball, over!" Stephen said.

We were so wrapped up with what was going on that we failed to notice Greyhaired walking down the road! When we spotted him, my brother Mark and I looked at each other in surprise.

"Is it still all clear, over?" Stephen's voice snapped us back into focus…

"Yes, Stephen, it's still all clear, it is all clear, over!" we replied, trying our hardest not to laugh!

Greyhaired opened his front door and went in... suddenly we heard a bit of shouting and commotion over the radio.... then Greyhaired came rushing out of his front door, holding a long length of wood in his hands. Stephen suddenly came racing out from the passageway by the side of Greyhaired's house. He ran so fast and in such a panic, that he didn't seem to notice the length of wood that Greyhaired broke across his legs – Stephen just ran straight through it! We all ran off down the road. We laughed and laughed. Stephen didn't seem to be too impressed... But he had rescued the ball! It was mission accomplished!

I remember that one day I was sat on the roof of the shed in our back garden. It was a great place to sit and think, or just to lie back and enjoy looking up into the clouds. As I was enjoying the sunshine, I suddenly noticed a plume of smoke arising from our neighbours' house who lived over the road, at the bottom of our garden. Their house was on fire! Then I remember seeing a figure running down the road towards the house- it was my Dad! Whilst other people were stood there just watching, without any hesitation, he ran up the path that led to the house, kicked open the front door and raced inside. Moments later, he emerged with the family, and got them to safety, until the Fire Brigade arrived. He never took any credit, no one thanked him and he really didn't want to talk about it, but he saved their lives. That was my Dad...my hero!

As a child I was always getting hurt. Once, when I was about three years old, I remember climbing up onto my parent's window sill in their bedroom, to see the painter and decorator painting the outside of our next- door neighbours house. I opened the window to say "Hello", when suddenly I felt two hands on my back, that pushed me straight out of the window, only to fall about twenty feet onto the concrete path. My sister, Linda, admitted years later that she was the culprit.

Once, as I was buying an ice cream from the van that often came down our road, it pulled away before I had received my ice cream, and so I jumped and grabbed onto the counter on the side of the van. The boy that had served me grabbed my hands and yanked them from off of the counter and so I fell, landing with my arm outstretched, and the van's rear wheel running over it, narrowly missing my head!

Many times, I would climb trees to get the conkers, only to fall out, usually breaking my arm. One time, I fell out of a conker tree, knocking myself out, resulting in a short stay in hospital, in which I had to use a wheelchair to get around. Four times my arm was in plaster as a boy and every time I noticed that I always developed an itch under the plaster, and it was always in the place that you couldn't get to… Knitting needles and other such implements were employed in the attempt to scratch the itch, but it always remained out of reach.

Once, whilst playing chase, I slipped and fell on a broken milk bottle, cutting my wrist very deeply and exposing the tendons, which ended up needing eight stitches. Even though I had many knocks and falls, I never had a sense of danger in the things that I did. The Bible says that "Foolishness is bound in the heart of a child…" (Proverbs 22:15) and I did many foolish things, not fearing what might happen to me. Fun was the name of the game!

Vision of Eternity

God was not someone that I really paid too much attention to, or gave much thought about. When it would thunder, I thought that God was moving His furniture around. If I did ever think about God, the same image would always come into my mind- that of a young boy, wearing a school uniform of blue shorts and a red v-neck jumper, laying down with His hands under His chin, and just lazily watching life go by on planet Earth. Certainly not a God to be feared.

Then one day, a mobile Dentist van pulled up at our school. We were all to have our teeth checked out by the dentist and then, if necessary, have a follow-up appointment if we needed any treatment.

I was appointed to have a tooth out, so I found myself settling back into the dentists' chair. Now in those days, when a child needed a tooth pulled out, they would give them gas, not an injection. They stopped the practise of gassing children to sleep because sometimes, they would give them too much gas and gas them to death.

" Ok, count backwards from three…" said the dentist, as he placed the mask over my nose and mouth. The smell of the gas reminded me of the glue that my brothers and I would use to make model aeroplanes with, a very sharp and overwhelming smell. "Three…two…one…" I counted, then suddenly I was no longer in the dentist's van. I was no longer sat in his chair. I found myself in Eternity. How did I know that it was Eternity? I don't know, I just knew that it was. It was black. It was vast. It stretched from my right side into nothingness. It stretched on my left side into nothingness. I didn't have a physical body, but I was fully conscious. I was overwhelmed by a feeling of desolation, abandonment, isolation.

Suddenly I saw in front of me a flat plateau of a rock that descended down into nothingness. On the rock, kneeling, was a little boy. He was crying with his face cupped in his hands. I knew that the little boy was me. As I was watching the scene, there suddenly appeared from the right side, a shaft of brilliant white light from out of the darkness and it shone on the boy on the rock, and at once I found myself waking up in the dentist's chair, minus one tooth! I had no idea what had happened. I did not know what the experience meant. I didn't tell anyone about it because it all seemed a bit strange and I didn't want to be ridiculed about it. Little did I know that twenty- five years later, I would have another encounter with that Light...

That experience, as strange as it was, didn't do much to change my ways. I was still growing up in much sin. In my early teens I developed a real passion for Martial Arts that was to last for the next twenty years of my life! I studied Ninjitsu, a very nasty form of Martial Arts. I would attend courses all over the country. It wasn't unusual for the practise of black magic to be a part of the programme on the courses that I attended.

One time the Leaders had invited a witch to come and teach us about healing. Now I was sceptical about it all until one of the men, who I had befriended on the course, volunteered to be healed of an ailment that he told the group he had had for quite a while. The woman got him to lay on a table and did some hocus pocus type of thing over him, when he suddenly jumped off of the table claiming to be totally healed!

On another occasion, there was a demonstration of this dark power. A man kneeled down on the floor, being blindfolded, whilst another man stood behind him with a sword raised above his head. Without any warning, the man struck downwards with the sword, and the man kneeling down suddenly rolled to the side and avoided any harm. This was all done silently without any communication between the two men involved. (I saw for myself that there was a real power behind black magic.)

I studied how to kill people. How to kill them quickly and quietly. My arsenal of weapons increased to knives, samurai swords, chains, throwing stars, hand claws, to name but a few. I had a lot of deadly weapons and I knew how to use them. This gave me a huge sense of power, of confidence, knowing that I could defend myself, if ever I needed to. Yet inside, I still felt so insecure. There was a fear deep down inside of me. I knew that, deep inside, I really didn't want to hurt anyone, but that was a weakness in the eyes of a warrior.

On one of the training courses, which was held in an old Naval Training Base, near Ipswich, we were given a demonstration by the SAS on Hostage Extraction. The SAS were regular attendees on the courses that I went to because the training wasn't sport orientated like other Martial Arts, but they were practical on how to kill (I got to train with the SAS regularly, and with many other Special Forces from many different countries.)

We were led to an old, abandoned building, and ushered up one flight of stairs into a large room. The corner of the room had been taped off with hazard tape to create a safety area, where we were told to stand, and given strict instructions not to cross the tape, because our safety could not be guaranteed if we did! There were three chairs lined up against a wall, with a door to the right of them. On the middle chair sat a man, blindfolded and with his hands tied behind his back. On the chairs that were either side of him were china plates positioned as targets, representing terrorists. After a brief explanation of the typical procedure of hostage rescue, the SAS team left the room. Then we waited…

It grew very tense as minutes passed by, waiting, not knowing what was going to happen. And still we waited. People started looking at each other, questioning what was going on. Was there a problem? Suddenly there was a huge explosion, and the door to the right of the man sitting on the chair, flew open!

Everyone's attention was immediately focused on that door, when suddenly, the other door by which we had entered into the room, burst open and in dived three men, rolling across the floor, shooting as they rolled, with the china plates exploding into pieces , as another man ran into the room, got hold of the man sitting on the chair, and with the help of one of his colleagues , dragged him out of the room and downstairs into a waiting car, which roared off down the road. The whole thing lasted less than ten seconds…

(Years later, when phoning my old Instructor, he told me that he had become a "Born Again" Believer in Jesus Christ, after having an "experience" after the death of a mutual friend, Derry. Derry was a lovely man, a Royal Marine Commando, with a big moustache and an even bigger smile! Apparently, whilst performing a demo of Hostage Rescue, someone had left a live round in his gun and Derry was shot in the stomach and killed.)

You can imagine my excitement when my father (who had not told me that he was an ex-SAS soldier) asked me to help him blow up the next-door neighbour's car! My father had grown tired of the neighbour parking in his parking space, and so the natural remedy was to destroy his car! Now I had a friend whose brother worked in a quarry, so I paid him to get us a stick of dynamite. When he gave it to me, I was a bit disappointed, it seemed a bit small, but he reassured me that it would do the trick.

So my Father explained what I should do- at three o'clock in the morning, I was to go out with the dynamite, and one potato, pull the fuse out, to lengthen it so it would give me more time to get back indoors before it exploded, light the fuse, throw it up the exhaust pipe, then jam the potato over the end of the exhaust and " Boom!"

So, at three o'clock I was up and dressed all in black. I crept downstairs and out of the front door and made my way to the car as quietly as an alley cat. I had the dynamite, the potato, the matches- it was all systems "Go!" I was just about to light the fuse, when I noticed that the cars' windows were a bit steamed up! Now, that was strange, because it wasn't a cold night, so I peeped inside the car, only to see that the next-door neighbours' lodger was sound asleep on the back seat. Abandon mission! I quickly made my way back in doors. I thought about what might have happened if I hadn't stopped to check inside of the car... I sighed a huge sigh of relief. Looking back now, I know that Someone had protected me from seriously injuring my neighbour.

A New Love

I continued over the years to study Ninjitsu. It was my first love until there came a love rival into my life in the form of a short, red headed young lady named Rachel. My brother Mark had taken a shine to Rachel's best friend, and had asked her out on a date. She agreed on one condition, that my brother would bring someone for Rachel, to which he agreed and I was nominated for the job! It was love at first sight.

I had said to my brother, Mark, many times that (being a bit of a joker back then) before I died, there were two things that I wanted to see...one, an African who was bad at dancing, and two, a good-looking red-head. I had seen the first, and now, standing before me was the completion of my lifetime's ambition! We arranged to go out to a nightclub the following week. It was 5th February, 1988. We have been together ever since.

One day, Rachel and I had been out for a drive and as we pulled up outside my house, I saw my sister, Linda, standing in the window, reading a book. Now I hadn't seen Linda for years because she had cut herself off from the family due to some issue that she had from her teenage years. When Rachel saw her, she said "she's reading the Bible!" I thought to myself, "how on earth can you tell that it's a Bible she's reading?" but, sure enough, it was a Bible! I noticed that, although it was a clear day with a lovely blue sky, there was a huge grey cloud just hanging over our house.

As I entered the house, my brother Mark said, "there's something weird going on! Linda keeps saying that the devil is after her, and as she said that, the front door just blew open!" It wasn't windy outside. It was a bit too freaky for me, so Rachel and I went upstairs to my bedroom. I had a punch bag hung up in my room and we were going to do some Kickboxing training.

After about an hour, as we were in my room, I suddenly became aware of an overpowering smell of roses! It was as if my mother had come into the room with her air freshener spray, as she would do, and had given it a good blast. I had to see where that smell was coming from, and so as I opened my bedroom door I was surprised to see there a small man, dressed in black, standing outside of my door. He looked at me, turned to the left and walked down the passageway into my parents' bedroom.

"What on earth is happening?" I said to myself. Then a woman came out of the room and came up to me and explained that they were Christians who had come to pray for my sister. "I can see that you are under the INFLUENCE!" she said (meaning that she could see an evil presence in me.) I had to try and control myself, but anger was starting to boil up…I didn't know where that smell came from, no one was burning any incense or waving a censer around, or anything that would create such a powerful smell.

I went into my parents' room, and there on the bed was my sister, Linda, jabbering and speaking all sorts of weird things. I turned to the Christians that were there and started to use some foul language to express my objection to who they were and what they were doing. As I tried to talk to Linda, that overwhelming smell of roses filled the room again! But this was a different room. I turned to Rachel and said "can you smell that smell? Where is it coming from?"

I spent all that night, sat on the sofa holding my sister's hand because she was too afraid to close her eyes. I didn't know it at the time, but the Christians were trying to deliver my sister from the powers of darkness that were clearly oppressing her. It was one of the scariest things that I had witnessed. I learned from the Bible that Jesus is called The Rose of Sharon. That explained the smell of roses. He was there.

Rachel and I were married six years after we had met, and were blessed with four wonderful children- Keeleigh, Joseph, Joel and Isaac. We had a fifth child, a boy named Samuel, but one night, as I lay in bed, trying to sleep, I had a vision, just like an ultra-sound picture, of a baby in the womb, curled up. Then suddenly a brilliant, white light shone on the child, and he was enveloped in radiant light.

The next day, on arriving home from work, Rachel told me that she had had a miscarriage. The doctors were a bit perplexed by it because after they had examined Rachel, they said that there were pregnancy hormones in her blood, yet they could see no trace of a pregnancy in her womb! It was hard to feel sad, because I knew where Samuel had gone....

Looking back on my childhood and growing up, I always had a sense of being protected. Bad things seemed to happen to other people, not to me, and even if they did, they didn't seem to have any lasting effect upon me. I was always in the right, in my own eyes. I loved to argue. Whatever I did, I would easily justify my actions and motives to myself. I was a joker, who could never take anything seriously. In fact, someone once said about me that they found it hard to talk to me because I couldn't have a serious conversation.

I was and am, always grateful to my parents' example that they showed to me. By example, my father showed me what it was to be a husband and a father. My mother showed me what a wife and a mothers' role is. They both sacrificed their lives for their children. They provided a stable, loving environment for me to grow up in.

I can honestly say that, looking back, I had the best childhood any child could have...

Thank you, Dad and Mum.

CHAPTER 2 ~ THE WORLD NEEDS TO KNOW!

" ...Go ye into all the world, and preach the gospel to every creature." - Mark 16:15

Now the good Lord knows how to redeem the worst times in your life and turn them into a blessing. This is exactly what He did through the birth of my second child, Joseph. It was at this time of my life that we had just found out that a close member of the family was a heroin addict, who had nearly died of an overdose. My sister-in-law's first child was born blind and autistic. I had been diagnosed with a rare chest disease, and so the events of Joseph's birth were the straw that broke the camel's back!

It was New Year's Eve when Rachel and I went to the John Radcliffe Hospital, in Oxford, to have the first scan of our second child. We were, as all parents are, filled with joy and excitement at the prospect of seeing our second child via ultra-sound. Rachel's first pregnancy had been such a blessed time, resulting in the birth of Keeleigh our daughter.

"There seems to be a thickening of skin on the back of the neck" said the nurse that was performing the ultra-sound. My immediate reaction inside was "So what?" "It is an indication of Downs Syndrome..." she said. "Oh, no! not Downs Syndrome. Anything but that!" was my reaction, due to my childhood memories of Terry Doe, a huge boy that lived near us.

He had Downs Syndrome and was kept hidden away in his house, and when he would break out, he would run and grab the nearest child, and pick them up and shake them like a rag doll. He meant no harm, he was just so joyful to see other children, but as a child, to me, he was terrifying. Now I was to be the parent of a "Terry Doe!"

The counsellor that was assigned to counsel us (I will call her " Counsellor Coldheart")was a very wicked and evil woman. Her whole aim was for us to have an abortion. All the information that she gave to us was of a negative view of Downs Syndrome, pointing out all of the possible problems one could face with such a child. She was trying to create a huge problem, and then dangle the carrot of abortion in front of our eyes.

Praise God for His mercy, for Rachel started to pray, and receive answers to her prayers. I was a mess, I didn't know what to do. But by the grace of God, when we got away from all the medical people, we realised that we were talking about our son, a human being, not a fashion accessory that you threw away because it didn't look a particular way.

When we told Counsellor Coldheart that we were going ahead with the pregnancy, she went berserk! She had already booked the bed for the "termination"(rather than call it " murder" for that is what it truly is.) But we had made up our minds, and no amount of emotional pressure or manipulation was going to change the course we had chosen. When I first told my mother about how Joseph was to be born, she immediately said "John, you know that no matter what, he will be loved!" It was just what I needed to hear…

I was sat up in bed one night trying to think of a name for our son. Now I hated the name Joseph. After Rachel had given birth to Keeleigh, she joined a Young Mothers group. One of the women there had named her son Joseph, and whenever she called his name out loud I would cringe on the inside. But as I was musing on certain names, a Voice spoke to me inside my head, "You'll call his name Joseph" It said. Without even thinking to question where the Voice came from, I repeated the name out loud, "Joseph" and as I did, it seemed to me to be the most beautiful name that ever there was! (Now children born with Downs Syndrome are born with an extra chromosome, and the name "Joseph" means "God adds one").

Joseph's Early Arrival

It wasn't the first time that I had heard this Voice. When I was into Heavy Metal music, I would go to the pub with a group of long haired friends of my sister-in -law. Now one of them was an Irish man. He had been involved with the IRA. My father hated the Irish, especially the IRA. His prejudices had rubbed off on me. I hated this man, for no reason. He hadn't done anything to me, except he had short hair! But every time he opened his mouth, I wanted to fill it!

Then once, as I was stood in the pub, looking daggers at this man, The Voice spoke to me "Do unto others as you would have them do unto you." Now, again, without bothering to question where such a Voice was coming from, I simply replied "I hate him, and I don't mind if he hates me, so I am treating him the way that I want him to treat me." You know, I could be a real jerk sometimes, even when talking to God.

At the time that Rachel was pregnant with Joseph, I was working in a factory, on a night shift. One night, whilst at work I got a phone call. All of the workers started shouting out "The baby is on the way!!" "Don't be ridiculous" I replied "He isn't due for another seven weeks." But they were right and I was wrong- Joseph was on his way!

The birth of Joseph was the most miraculous thing that I had ever seen! Unfortunately, Keeleigh had to be delivered by cesarean section, but Joseph was delivered naturally. We had eleven medical professionals in the delivery room, due to anticipated complications because children born with Downs Syndrome are usually born smaller than other children, but to be also born seven weeks early was a real concern to the medical team. Joseph was enormous! He had huge, wide shoulders, and weighed a healthy five pounds.

They questioned whether we had gotten his dates wrong because he was so big! He was rushed away to The Intensive Care Unit, where they could check him over and see if all was well. When we finally were allowed to see him later that night He was led there with a huge black eye! How he got that, we don't know, but one thing I did know, when I saw him, my heart just melted. All of the fear that I had, that I wouldn't be able to bond with him, or that I wouldn't be able to love him just melted away and I fell deeply in love with him.

He was kept in hospital for about seven weeks due to feeding problems, but eventually we were allowed to take him home. All was going well, until we started to notice that he couldn't keep his milk down. Every time he had milk he would be violently sick. But afterwards he would always be smiling! It wasn't long before he became dehydrated, and so we took him to the Doctors, who after examining him, pronounced that he was suffering from heart failure.

Now when Joseph was in the womb, they had scanned his heart because holes in the heart can be an issue relating to children with Downs Syndrome. They had found two holes in his heart. But they had told us that the holes would probably heal as Joseph grew up.

It looked like that wasn't going to be the case with Joseph, as he was rushed to the John Radcliffe Hospital. He had to have emergency open heart surgery. He was only two months old.

I couldn't go home and leave him in the hospital by himself and so arrangements were made by the staff to allow me to stay in a room for a week whilst Joseph recovered. No words in the world can describe the pain of seeing my two- month old son, laying in Intensive Care, with tubes coming out from everywhere, hooked up to all kinds of machines, with a huge cut from below his throat to the bottom of his chest. Knowing that his life depended on the machines. It simply broke my heart. But I had to push the hurt down inside so that I could deal with what was in front of me.

I would go in to see him early in the morning and there would be a wonderful Irish nurse there. I would go and see him in the afternoon and the same nurse would be there. I would go and see him in the evening and the same nurse would be there. I would go in to see Joseph in the early hours of the following morning and the same nurse was there! She told me that she worked a thirty-six hour shift. (I figured that the Irish people weren't so bad after all.)

When I would visit Joseph, I would stand gazing at him, and in my head, many, many times was a song playing. It was from a Kate Bush song "Running up that hill." It was only one particular line of the song that played in my head, over and over and over again…

"And if I only could, I'd make a deal with God, and I'd get Him to swap our places…" Oh! How I would have given anything to have been able to swap places with my son. I wanted it to be me in the bed, with the tubes and the scars, and for my boy to be pain free and healthy. I didn't realize it at the time, but the Lord was showing me through those circumstances that, that is what God did for me through His Son, Jesus Christ, because of His love for me, when He sent Jesus to die on the cross for my sins. How Christ became a substitute for me and suffered in my place so that I didn't need to suffer and die, but that I could be reconciled back to God and have eternal life.

But God was the last person that I wanted to hear about…

To my amazement, Joseph was out of hospital after eight days, still smiling as always! It was wonderful to have him back home and to see him making a full recovery. Out of gratitude to the people who cared for him, I organized a fund- raising event, by having my head shaved, and inviting my family and friends to come and support me. The local press came as well, and they did a little article for the local newspaper.

Things seemed to be settling back down to normal, when one day, I noticed that Joseph's left eye seemed to look a little bit cloudy. I hadn't noticed it before, but there was definitely something there, and so I took him to the doctors, who recommended us to the eye specialist in Oxford.

The consultant was a lovely South African man who had a genuine love for his patients. I will call him Mr Kindheart. He had a reassuring voice and red, rosy cheeks. After examining Joseph, Mr Kindheart told us that Joseph had been born with Congenital Glaucoma and was almost blind in his left eye, and that the pressure was building up fast in his eyes, and that he needed immediate surgery to save his sight.

My heart was at breaking point again, as Joseph was put to sleep and whisked away to theatre. I had to push the pain down and deal with what was in front of me. I sat thinking "Why? Why is this happening to my son? What has Joseph ever done to deserve such things?" As I sat in the waiting room, I noticed a Bible sat on the shelf. I took it down and opened it. I don't know why I did, but I did. But I soon put it back after a short time. It didn't speak to me. I didn't find any comfort in it. It just seemed dead and empty.

The surgery was a complete success, and so we were allowed to take Joseph home. We had regular appointments after that, which involved me holding Joseph on my lap to try and keep him calm whilst they gassed him to sleep. It was horrible. I was miserable. As they would take Joseph to theatre, I would make my way to the canteen and drown my sorrows in a full-English breakfast and countless cups of tea! Eventually though, everything seemed to settle down, and after about a year all things were well...

Farmer Evangelist

Then one Christmas time, we were invited by some local folk to a Carol Service at the local village hall. It was a lovely candle-lit evening, and afterwards I got talking to a local farmer, who was also a Christian and one of the organizers of that night's events. I will call him Farmer Evangelist. He was a young and very handsome man.

Now, I had recently developed an interest in Metal Detecting, and so I was very keen to get to know Farmer Evangelist, as he had land in the village that I could detect on. It was good land, too! It was well known amongst the Metal Detecting community that Great Bedwyn, where I lived, was premium detecting land. So, after asking Farmer Evangelist if I could detect on his land, I was pleasantly surprised by his readiness to agree.

So, he gave me his phone number and told me to give him a call, so that we could meet up and he would show me the land on which I could detect on. I was very excited! About a week later we met up and he took me in his Landrover over the fields, showing me where and where I couldn't detect. He parked up and we started chatting. He jokingly said "I'd better warn the Gamekeeper to look out for you so that he doesn't try to run you off the land!" "Just tell him to look out for the man who looks like Jesus!" I replied (due to the fact that I had long hair at that time.)

Now, Farmer Evangelist, being a Christian, had obviously asked the Lord for an opening to share the Gospel with me, and I, not knowing, had just opened the door wide and said "Come on in!" because he immediately asked me "How do you know what Jesus looked like?" and for the next two hours, he bombarded me with the Gospel!

When I got back home, Rachel asked me how it went, "He's a fanatic! "I said and relayed to her all that had happened. The way this man spoke about Jesus, with such a passion and deep conviction, scared me. He seemed like a crazy man on the loose. But deep down, I remember thinking, "If only I could believe what he believes, in the way he believes it!" He seemed so certain that God existed and that he was going to Heaven when he died.

I was envious of him, and yet terrified of him at the same time. Farmer Evangelist would phone me and talk about Jesus down the phone. I would hold the phone away from my ear so that I couldn't hear too much of what he was saying, puncturing his conversation every now and then with a "Oh, yeah... yeah... I see...yeah..." all the while, looking at Rachel and shaking my head.

He invited me to a Gentleman's Breakfast, and before I could say "No!" I said "Yes!" I have no idea where that "Yes!" came from. The last thing I wanted to do was to sit down with this man, and others like him, and have breakfast. But I went because I've always wanted to be a man of my word. I had said that I would go, and go I would even if I didn't like it...

When I arrived, I was treated like nobility! I had never felt so much love before from people who never even knew me. They served me. I saw women, meek and gentle, serving the men as if it was the most blessed thing to do. I was amazed. I had never seen anything like it before! Something inside of me was starting to stir.

Then, just before we were to eat, Farmer Evangelist stood up and said "Let us say grace" and continued to pray. Wow! I felt uncomfortable praying to a God who I knew that, if He existed, I had big issues with. I felt like a hypocrite as the words spilled out of my mouth. After it had ended, I went home vowing that I would have nothing more to do with this man. I would avoid him at all costs. But little did I know that, something had been stirred deep down inside of me…

The rage didn't manifest itself immediately, it came on gradually and got worse and worse. Inanimate objects were no longer safe in my house!

One day the dog flap wasn't working properly, and so, whilst trying to fix it, I got frustrated and punched it out and through the door! The Lawnmower wouldn't work, and so it ended up being a flying lawnmower! yes, it became a literal " Flymo",all the way down to the bottom of the garden! I could feel anger and rage bubbling up inside of me, and I didn't know how to deal with it.

I started to buy bottles of beer and keep them at home so that I could have a drink to try and calm myself down. I started dabbling with "soft" drugs to try to calm the storm that was starting to rage inside of me. I had made arrangements with a friend of mine to travel to Bournemouth, with the intent of doing some harder drugs.

All of the pressure, stress and pain of the lasts few years had started to leak out of me in violent outbursts. I was afraid, not for myself, but for the people around me. I knew that someone would say or do the wrong thing to me, and I would kill them with my bare hands, where they stood. I knew how to do it, and now I wished that I didn't… I said to my Mother, who had come over to babysit, "Mum, the next time that you see me, I will either be in prison or in an Asylum." She knew that I was at breaking point, and she expressed her concerns for me.

Rachel and I had recently finished going to Kickboxing classes, which we had been attending for a number of years, because the Instructor had moved out of the area. So, Rachel and her sister, Nicola, had decided to try Yoga. I went to one lesson but fell asleep halfway through! I decided that it was a bit too girly for me. Eventually the Yoga classes were also cancelled, and so it left Rachel seeking something else to take an interest in.

One of the women that lived in our village also had a son with Downs Syndrome. She was a Christian. She invited Rachel to an Alpha Course, which was run by the local Anglican Church. It was a course that explained Christianity and the issues of life.

I had never heard of an Alpha Course before and so when Rachel asked me if I would like to come to one of the meetings, I replied " No thanks, I'm not interested in computers." "No!" she said, "It's a course about Christianity." "WHAT!!" I snapped back. The growling beast was stirred inside....

Rachel, who knew me inside and out, replied "You have a chance to argue with them, and there is free food!" Two things that I loved- to argue and to eat! When I was growing up, I would deliberately disagree with people so that I could argue with them. My Mother was always saying to me "You love to argue!" And I did. I would argue that black was white, and I would never back down even if I knew that I was in the wrong. I was trained to never back down... NEVER.

So, I decided that I would go and sort out these deluded Christians and show them how wrong they all were.

How wrong I was! God had other ideas...

One of the other reasons that I agreed to go to the Alpha Course was that it was to be held in a school and not in a church. I didn't want to step inside of a church. No way! When we arrived, I was quite shocked at how many people were there. I thought that it would be just a few old folk, sat around sharing knitting patterns and recipes, etc but it wasn't. There were many people there of my age. Younger than me. Couples, old and young.

I took my place at one of the tables in the hall and tried to blend in with the background. Eventually a grey -haired man stood up to speak. I will call him "Humbleman" because he dressed like an ordinary man, and acted like an ordinary man, but I later found out that he was a millionaire and moved in high society!

He waffled on for what seemed like an eternity! I don't remember what he said, but what really shocked me was that Humbleman, at one point, had to stop speaking momentarily, to catch himself from crying when talking about his Heavenly Father. He actually believed what he was saying! I could see it in his actions and expressions on his face. I couldn't believe it...Another crazy man!

Then he started talking about how much God loved ME...The beast rose up from inside. "How dare he say that God loves me! ...God loves me? Really? He has a funny way of showing it! allowing all of this stuff to happen to me..." The anger started to boil, and my knuckles were turning white. "Just one punch, that's all I would need, just one punch to lay him out straight" I thought as I was trying my hardest to control myself.

Rachel kept turning around and looking at me. "Stop heavy breathing! " she said, as the hot breath forced its way out of my nostrils like a bull seeing a red rag! Eventually, Humbleman stopped speaking and sat down. I needed to eat something and calm down before we broke off into groups to "discuss" what was said...

After the meal we were divided up into small groups. We went into a side room and sat down. There were about eight of us, with a married couple appointed to answer our questions. I was ready. I asked my question, ready to argue with whatever answer was given-it didn't matter what it was.

I wanted to unleash some of the anger that was built up in me. But every time I asked a question, the couple would answer with such humility, gentleness and wisdom that it just took the wind out of my sails! This wasn't fair. Instead of arguing, I found myself listening. I left the meeting feeling very annoyed with myself having not argued with them at all! So, I decided that I would go back the following week...

The more of the course that I attended, the more that I heard answers to life, and especially, to my life. It seemed as though the whole course was structured just to answer my questions! The rage inside of me had seemed to have calmed. I started to enjoy listening to Humbleman's preaching.

I witnessed the same love amongst these Christians as I had seen amongst Farmer Evangelist and his crew at the Gentleman's Breakfast. But I just couldn't understand the Gospel. It made no sense. How can a Man, dying on a cross two thousand years ago, help me today?

We were invited to attend a church service on a Sunday. The only time that I'd been in church before was as a boy, to a couple of weddings, and to the funeral of one of my cousins. I was very self- conscious as I entered the church.

Immediately, one of the older Christian women spotted me and came over and gave me a great, big hug! " Ahhhh! Get away from me, what are you doing?" were the silent protests in my head. Now, as a Martial Artist, there is a boundary line that people just don't step across, unless they want to put themselves in danger.

But this woman just invaded my safety zone with her love, and I just couldn't stand it! I felt vulnerable. I might have shown some emotion in public, and that would just not do! I forced a smile at her, and made my way in the opposite direction, all the while keeping her in the corner of my vision. No stranger had ever hugged me before. I wondered what they were after?

I was working as a Postman at this time. I would get up at 3:45 am in the morning and drive to work at around 4:30 am. I loved being up at that time. It was so peaceful and the roads were always empty. One morning, as I was driving to work, I had the radio on. I was listening to a song. The lyrics went like this;

"… You don't even know me, you say that I'm not living right. You don't understand me, so why do you judge my life?"

The Voice spoke to me…." That's you, John!" It said. Now I was very proud of the fact that I could judge someone within a few minutes of meeting them. Whether they were good or bad (usually they were judged to be bad.) I would have them pigeon holed into one of my little boxes.

To my absolute amazement, I spoke out of my mouth, "Yes, you're right, that is me, and I AM WRONG to do it!" The shock of hearing those words coming from out of my own mouth nearly caused me to crash the car!

I pulled over and stopped to think. Yes, that was me, I did judge people and I really didn't like being that way. I was wrong, and for the first time in my life I had admitted it to myself! I never bothered to ask The Voice who He was that kept speaking to me. In a funny way, it just seemed as if that Voice had always spoken to me.

He Is Alive

The day came when it would be the last meeting of the Alpha Course. It was called The Holy Spirit day. The session was to be held, all day, at a Christian Retreat near Cirencester. It was to be held on a Saturday, which was a problem because I had to work, and I desperately wanted to attend. When the Saturday came, I was feeling very ill due to having developed a cold. I had said to Rachel that I would be home as soon as I could so that we could go together for the afternoon session. It was a bitterly cold, snowy morning, which added to my desire to get the mail delivered as soon as I could and to get back home into the warmth.

Rachel, Nicola and myself soon arrived at the venue. It was a beautiful, old barn, that had white walls and old oak beams. The lights seemed to be turned down low, so as to create a more relaxed atmosphere, I supposed. We found some empty seats and sat down to listen. Humbleman was teaching about the Holy Spirit- who He was and what He does. I cannot remember much of what was said. Even though the Voice had spoken to me on various occasions and things in my life had been so clearly arranged, I just couldn't grasp why the Christians worshipped a God who was confined to the pages of a book!

It soon drew near to the end of the meeting, and Humbleman invited anyone that needed prayer or that wanted to give their life to Jesus, to find the Prayer Teams that were dotted around the room, who would pray for them. As I sat there, the conflict began..." A book cannot help you...The Bible is not true, it's just a bunch of fairy stories... this God is not real...don't go up for prayer, you'll look a fool...everyone will see that you need help and they will think that you are weak. You're strong enough to cope with life by yourself...you don't need God!" were the things that a different voice was saying to me...

Isn't that exactly the same voice that you have heard, my friend?

"But I have to know!" I said to the tormenting voice in my head." If it's not true, then there is no hope!" I mourned. As I sat there, I was reminded of New Years' Eve, when, whilst high on drugs and alcohol, I went out into my friend's back garden, and at the stroke of midnight I looked up into the starry sky and said "God, if you are real, I want to make my peace with You!" Eleven months later, God was about to answer that prayer.

Again, I said in my heart, as I sat there struggling, not knowing what to do, " Jesus, if You are real, if You can forgive me and take away all of my pain and anger, if You can heal my broken heart today, not tomorrow, not in a few years' time. If You can do it today, I'll know that You are real and I will follow You all the days of my life." I suddenly found myself standing in line for prayer. "What are you doing, you fool? Everyone can see that you are weak!" repeated the accusing voice, but I kept saying to myself "I've got to know if it's true… I've got to know."

It was a couple from my village that prayed for me. They had been praying for Rachel and myself for a few years. The Christian lady who first invited Rachel to the Alpha Course had told them about us having a son with Downs Syndrome, and they had prayed for us without knowing who we were, and now, here I was, without knowing them, about to be prayed for. How God arranges these things is amazing!

The man asked me my reasons for needing prayer. After a very brief summary of my issues, he spoke. "Repeat after me" he said and continued to say a prayer. As I did I suddenly thought "I must be mad! I'm standing here for all the world to see, saying these words that I don't believe…" As I was in conversation with myself, I had my eyes closed.

Suddenly a speck of brilliant, white light started to appear in the top, right hand corner of my vision. It grew bigger and bigger and spread all the way across my vision. It was so bright, that even with my eyes closed, I started to flinch at the intensity of the light. I snapped open my eyes, thinking that I would see someone shining a light in my face, but there was no one there! I was staring into a grey brick wall, with no light source, and no reflection. The room was still dimly lit. "What on earth is going on?" I asked myself as I closed my eyes again, only to see that, on the inside, it was still brilliantly light!

Then it was as if my eyes pivoted downwards and I could see inside of my body, that I was filled with this amazing, white Light. Then it felt like someone came up from behind me and lifted off a huge weight from off of my shoulders. I felt so light on my feet, that my heels left the floor!

The man next to me put his hand on my shoulder. If he hadn't, I felt like I would have floated up to the ceiling! It felt like someone had opened the top of my skull and had poured in knowledge.

Suddenly, I knew that the Bible was the truth from beginning to end. I knew that there was a God. And I knew that JESUS WAS ALIVE! "He's alive!" I said to myself, "He really is alive!" I was shocked because I had taken His Name in vain so many times, and now as I stood in His presence, all I felt was His love! "The world needs to know!" I said as I realised the truth about Jesus Christ. A tear trickled down the side of my face as the man asked me how I felt? "Lighter!" was my reply. I walked outside.

I felt like I had just been run over by a train. I sat down on a bench and looked around. Everything was new. I said to myself, as I looked up into a brand new sky "Wow! Look at the sky, it's so blue!" Then I diverted my gaze to the ground "And look at the grass, each individual blade is so unique yet they are all the same!" I looked at my hand, the way that the skin stretched and folded as I opened and closed it, and just marvelled at the amazing piece of engineering that was my hand!

I stopped and said to myself "Is this insanity? Have I gone over the edge? If it is, I don't want to be healed!" I felt brand new! I had no idea what had happened to me, I didn't have any Bible knowledge, and so I knew nothing about the Rebirth (or, being Born Again, as it is also known) but whoever that was that went into that barn on that day was dead, and whoever it was that came of that barn on that day had a new life...

CHAPTER 3 ~ LEARNING TO WALK

" As newborn babes, desire the sincere milk of the Word, that ye may grow thereby..." - 1Peter 2:2

I really had no clue what had happened to me in that barn. All I knew was that I had met with the risen Christ, and He had touched me, changed me and had made me new. Now I had a hunger for His Word, the Holy Bible. It wasn't a thought like..." Oh well! Now that I'm a Christian, I'd better read the bible!" No! It was a HUNGER for His Word.

So, I got a Bible and started to read. It was amazing! I remember that I kept closing the Bible so that I could look at the cover that said in gold letters "Holy Bible", to make sure that it was the Bible that I was reading, because this book had changed! When, in the past, I had tried to read it, it was simply dead and I couldn't understand it. But now it had come to life. When I say that it had come to life, that's exactly what I mean- as I would read it, the Lord would speak to me through it, as if the Bible had been written just for me. The words had come to life.

I know that this may sound weird, but as I held the Bible and looked at it, I could see it breathing! I would sit down, and there would be a question in my head, something about God or about life. I would open the Bible to read it, and "Boom!" there was the answer, right before my eyes! This happened time and time again...

I really didn't know who I was anymore. I knew that I had changed on the inside. Things that I loved before were now detestable to me. I used to love Metallica, a heavy metal rock band. I was always listening to their music but now, I couldn't stand to hear it! It was horrible. My eyes and ears had been opened to spiritual things, and now I could see and hear that their music was all about death and the powers of darkness.

All of my Martial Arts equipment, my weapons and all of my clothing I just had to get rid of, so I got my kit bag, that was full of my weapons, and I put it into the car and drove to the local Police Station and handed them in and told them to destroy them all. My wife and I went to a local Car Boot Sale and set up a table and sold our music records, my Martial

Arts gear and any other thing that the Lord had shown us that was in our house that was not pleasing to Him. With the help of the Holy Spirit, we started in the attic, and went from the top to the bottom of our house, throwing out or selling anything that the Lord said to, regardless of its value, whether material or sentimental.

One day, whilst reading my Bible, I came across a verse in the third chapter of the Gospel according to John. In the third verse it says "…Except a man be born again, he cannot see the Kingdom of God." It hit me like a train! That's what had happened to me, that is exactly how I felt, "…born again!" The Bible also says that, "Therefore if any man be in Christ, he is a new creature: old things are passed away, behold, all things are become new." (2 Corinthians 5:17).

It is hard to try and explain or describe it to someone who is not Born Again, how this change affects you on the inside. It is a bit like trying to explain to someone who has never had children, what it's like to hold your new-born baby in your arms- it's beyond words, the only way to know is to experience it for yourself. Obviously, to those who know you, and they see this sudden change in your behaviour, they automatically think that you have gone crazy! I can understand it because the change in me was so radical. But then again, when I read the Bible, I saw that the Lord Jesus Christ was a radical in the way He lived, and even He was accused of being crazy!

The Lord also started to speak to me through my dreams. Looking back now, I could see that He was speaking to me through my dreams a long time before I was Born Again.

He has been speaking to you, whoever you maybe reading this book, through your dreams. The question is, have you been listening?

Dreams of Christ

In one of my dreams, I saw Christ. To be honest, it was so real, it was more like a vision, an actual experience! I was stood on a dusty patch of ground. Roman soldiers were walking to and fro. One walked right past me! I could see the beautiful scarlet of his cloak as it waved behind him n the wind. I caught a glimpse of the sunlight reflecting from off of his silver breastplate.

As he passed me, I looked down. There, on the dusty ground, was a rugged, weather beaten cross. Laying on the cross was Jesus. He was

31

looking straight at me! He gazed deeply into my eyes. He was looking at me with such an intense love, such a look of marvel on His face as He looked at me that, as they drove a nail through His wrist, He was unaware of the pain, because He was so captivated by me! It was like He was looking at the most amazing thing that He had ever seen! (Now, I don't want you to think it's because I'm so lovely, or I'm trying to make me out to be something extra special- it was just the way He was looking at me)

I was startled to think that He would look at me in such a way, knowing what a filthy pig I was and what I had done in my life! It was a gaze that I could never describe or never forget, but then it changed. Even though His expression on His face hadn't changed, the look in His eye had. He was now looking at me as if to say, "John, it was because of YOUR sin that I had to suffer in order to redeem you. It was because of YOUR sin that I had to shed my blood in order to wash you and make you clean." I felt so ashamed, guilty and humbled by that look.

The dream ended with someone being nailed to the cross by having a nail driven through their ear, which I thought was a weird ending to such a wonderful dream. I felt that it had somehow spoiled the dream.

When I awoke I realised for the first time that, my sin hadn't just hurt myself and the people around me, IT HAD HURT GOD HIMSELF! Because we are so self-centred, when we sin and things go wrong in our lives, or bad things happen to us, we shake our fists at God and blame Him! "Oh, if there's a God, why would He let this happen to me…?" It's because we live our lives our own way, away from God. We think we know better than Him.

It is like someone who is trying to cross a busy Motorway. You walk up to them and say, "Friend, let me give you some helpful advice" and you hand them an instruction booklet on how to cross the road safely. But, they turn around and say, "How dare you tell me what to do!" and they throw the booklet back in your face. They go to cross the Motorway, and "BAM!" they get hit by a truck… Please tell me, is it your fault that they rejected the wise counsel that you gave them, or is it their own fault for doing it their way? God has given us The Holy Bible that tells us how to live life so that we can be blessed. MY friend, it's not God's fault that something bad has happened to you. He is the solution, not the problem.

Soon after the dream, when I read my Bible, the Holy Spirit led me to read these verses from the book of Exodus;

"And if the servant shall plainly say, I love my Master, my wife and my children; I will not go out free: Then his Master shall bring him unto the judges; He shall also bring him to the door, or unto the door post; and his Master shall bore his ear through with an aul; and he shall serve Him forever."   (Exodus 21:5-6) I was amazed that such a thing was in the Bible! What a wonderful ending to my dream! The Lord was showing me that I would be His forever! Something that I thought was so weird had turned out to be such an amazing Word from the Lord! Oh! Lovely Jesus!

The Lord spoke to me again, in another dream. This time I dreamt that it was the end of the world- the Second Coming of Christ. It was dark in the dream, and I was standing outside of the church in Burbage, when suddenly there appeared a huge storm in the sky. There was lightning flashing all around. I went out into the road to get a better view of what was happening. People were running away from the direction of the storm.

They were all terrified, running past me in a panic, but I looked into the storm and knew that it was my Lord's coming, and so I ran towards the storm. As I approached the place from where the lightning was coming, the Lord Jesus stood there in front of me. I ran into His outstretched arms and as I did, a clear booming Voice spoke to me in my dream and said "You are saved!", and then I awoke with a sense of great joy and peace. I knew that He had spoken to me and given me an assurance that I had been truly saved!

Another time, not too long after this dream, just as I was falling asleep, suddenly a loud Voice spoke to me "You're different!" The Voice exclaimed. I awoke with a jump- I was startled, there was someone else in the bedroom! I looked around but there was no one there! Someone, a man's Voice had just spoken to me!

I lay there, in the dark, doing a mental check- it wasn't Rachel, because it was a man's Voice, and besides, she was fast asleep next to me. It wasn't any of my sons' voices calling for me, no It was a man's Voice. The strange thing was, was that, I was overwhelmed with a sense of peace, even though someone had just spoken in my ear, there was no fear inside of me, only peace. I lay there and knew that my Lord had just spoken to me- that I had actually heard His Voice! I didn't know what He meant by "You're different."

The next day I was reading my Bible (back then I read the NKJV of the

Bible. I am now an AKJV only man!). I was reading the Book of Numbers when I read this verse;

"But My servant Caleb, because he has a DIFFERENT spirit in him and has followed Me fully, I will bring into the land where he went, and his descendants shall inherit it." (Numbers 14:24) The word "Different" jumped off of the page and my heart started to race- I now knew what the Lord was saying to me, that I was to follow Him whole-heartedly! It was, and is, a very special word to me…

The Lord also confirmed this Word by the mouth of a Polish Pastor who I had brought to our house to meet my family whilst he was in our country, promoting his ministry. He had invited me to preach in his church in Poland, and whilst I was there talking to his wife, I told her this story about hearing His Voice and the scripture that He had confirmed it by. When the Pastor heard this he turned to his wife and said "Do you remember, that when I came back from England, that I told you about John, and that I said that he was DIFFERENT!" This was not to make me feel prideful or better than other people, but that the Lord was telling me that I had been converted and that I truly was a different man.

Bible Study-Living Waters

I was invited by a dear brother (the man who prayed for me at The Christian Retreat, when I met with the Lord,) to a Bible study that was to be held at his mother's house in the village. I readily agreed to go along. The house was a beautiful old cottage, with small rooms and low ceilings. There was a small group gathered and the meeting began with some praise and worship songs.

Then Paul, who was the preacher, along with his wife, Merle, began to teach from the book of Daniel. I really didn't like what he said. I was eager to leave at the end, vowing to myself that I would not be returning to any future meetings. You can imagine how surprised I was when, being invited to the next meeting, I instantly said "Yes!" I couldn't believe it! Where did that "Yes" come from? I was very annoyed with myself for agreeing to go, but I wanted to be a man of my word, and so when the time came for the next meeting, along I plodded, not really looking forward to it at all.

Now God is so lovely! He knows what is best for us, and He will direct our paths into the good things that He has in store for those who love Him. In my personal study of the scriptures, the Lord had highlighted a verse from the Gospel of John. In the seventh chapter, the thirty-eighth verse, it says;

"He that believeth on Me, as the scripture hath said, out of his belly shall flow rivers of living water."

As I sat through the second Bible study, with Paul, it was as if I was hearing a completely different preacher! He was still teaching from the book of Daniel, but I loved every minute of it! I was amazed at the change. I didn't understand why, the first time I hated it, but now, I loved it. I left feeling elated!

When I got to my house, I opened the front door (which opened straight into our living room) and I just stood in the doorway. Rachel was sat on the sofa. She looked up at me and asked "How did you get on?" but I didn't answer her because I was overwhelmed by the fact that I was aware that a river was flowing from out of my belly! (Now, before you think I'm crazy, my friend, it's a spiritual river, the Holy Spirit, not a literal river!) But I was rooted to the spot, wondering at this river flowing from me- it was such a marvellous experience!

Again, the Lord was showing me that His Word is the truth. These things are real. And these things can be experienced by all who are willing to believe!

Again, the Lord spoke to me through a powerful dream. I was in a room. It had no furniture in it, it was just a bare room. There was also someone else in the room, a well- dressed man. He looked like someone you would see in a photo from the early 1900s. He was wearing a very smart, black suit, a white shirt and tie. He was quite an elderly gentleman. As I looked at him, I started to notice that his behaviour was starting to change. He looked like he was becoming irritated by my presence.

Suddenly, he turned and started to rush towards me, lowering his forehead as he did. As he came towards me, I lowered my forehead, and rushed to meet him. We ran and clashed our foreheads together like a couple of stags fighting over territory on a mountain side! Then I awoke.

The Lord graciously gave me the interpretation. The elderly gentleman represented the Traditions of Men in the Church. He represented " Churchianity" a powerless religion based on the teachings, traditions and commandments of men. The Lord was showing me that I was to come against such things. Soon after this dream, I attended a Bible study in Marlborough, with Paul and Merle Williams, the faithful couple who had led the Bible study back in my village, Great Bedwyn. During the meeting, Merle approached me and told me that she had a word for me from the Lord.

"And He said unto me, son of man, get thee unto the house of Israel, and speak with My Words unto them. For thou art not sent to a people of a strange speech and of an hard language, but to the house of Israel: Not to many people of a strange speech and of an hard language, whose words thou canst not understand. Surely, had I sent thee to them, they would have hearkened unto thee. But the house of Israel will not hearken unto thee; for they will not hearken unto Me: for all the house of Israel are impudent and hardhearted. Behold, I have made thy face strong against their faces, and THY FOREHEAD STRONG AGAINST THEIR FOREHEADS. AS AN ADAMANT HARDER THAN FLINT HAVE I MADE THY FOREHEAD: fear them not, neither be dismayed at their looks, though they be a rebellious house." (Ezekiel 3:4-9)

Again, I was amazed that something like this was in the Bible. I was amazed at how God was speaking to me through my dreams.

Many people ask how God speaks to people, because they doubt the existence of God, and yet they have done nothing to try to search for God or to reach out to Him or if they have, it was only for a short period of time. God will speak through His Holy Word, the Bible. He will speak to people through dreams and visions.

It is commonly reported that many Muslims around the world are coming to faith in Jesus, because He has been appearing to them in their dreams and by visions. The Lord will also speak through His creation. He will also speak through the mouths of other people. The truth is, not that God doesn't speak, but that people do not take the time to listen. They are too wrapped up and distracted by the things of this world to bother with God, until something goes wrong in their lives, and then they want to find someone to blame, and they always want to place the blame upon God, whom they say doesn't exist!

To be born again opens you up to the reality of the Kingdom of Heaven. The spirit realm unfolds to you and becomes very real.

One day we were to attend the annual School Leavers Ceremony of the local school. It was an event that said "Goodbye! "to the children who were leaving Primary School to attend Secondary School in the Autumn.

The ceremony was held at the local church in Great Bedwyn, a church well known to be spiritually dead amongst the local Christians. Each child was presented with a Bible at the end of the ceremony. I was sat on the right side of the church. Even though it was packed, it still seemed empty. There was no presence of God there. I sat through the songs and speeches, inwardly begging for them to hurry up as my bottom was growing numb from sitting on the wooden pew.

Then it came to the part where they handed out the Bibles… "Not long now!" I thought to myself. As I glanced over my left shoulder, to watch the children receive their Bibles, suddenly an Angel appeared above the isle! He was holding a book in his hands and was busy writing the names of the children who were receiving Bibles, in his book. He was at an angle of about thirty degrees, looking downwards. He had shoulder length, straight reddish, golden hair and was wearing a white garment. I was amazed! As quickly as he appeared, he disappeared! "Who would of thought that you'd see an Angel in this place?" I thought to myself. God is full of surprises…

The Lord is no longer someone far away, but someone who is involved in our everyday life. Truly, The Lord really does want to be part of our lives and to help us in our time of need.

Many times, whilst working as a Postman, the Lord helped me. Joseph was still attending hospital appointments, and me, being a punctual man, I was always fighting against the clock at work, so that I could finish my round and go home in time to take Joseph to Oxford for his appointments. Some days didn't go the way that I had planned them to….

One day, Joseph had an appointment in Oxford. I was delivering mail on a large, rural round at work. This round I had done many times, and I knew that it would take me, at best, three and a half to four hours to complete and because of the appointment time, there wouldn't be any time to hang around! There were a few famous people that lived on this round, one of them being Frank Williams, owner of Williams Formula One Grand Prix.

On this particular morning I overslept! When I eventually arrived at work, most of the Posties had already left the Office. I threw the mail off as fast as I could, packed my pouches and loaded the van up with the mail. As I raced to the beginning of the round, I asked the Lord if He could slow time down so that I could get the round finished and back home to take Joseph to his appointment. I figured that, if He is God, He could do such things...It was impossible to do the Post round in the natural, there simply wasn't enough time. I did my best and left the rest up to the Lord.

Amazingly, I did the round in about two hours, which was impossible! But everything worked out perfectly, except that I was reported for driving too fast down Frank Williams driveway. Think about that, driving too fast for the owner of Williams Formula One! He should of signed me up!

As I read the scriptures and prayed, and as I listened to preachers and to my Bible study teachers, Paul and Merle, I realized that there was something else that the Lord wanted to give to me. A "Gift" the Bible calls it- the Baptism of The Holy Ghost. I had been baptised in water. The church that I was attending hired a mobile pool and had erected it in the Graveyard- a fitting place to be buried with Christ! Many people came to see myself and a sister in the Lord be baptised. It was a great day with games and a BBQ to accompany the baptismal ceremony.

I remember that after the baptism, a dear brother came up to me to congratulate me, so I held out my hand to shake his, but he said, "Ah! No! I'm going to give you a hug!" and wrapped his arms around me and gave me a huge hug. I was so shocked! I stood still and realised that I had never been hugged by a man in my life, not even by my dear father. I was thirty- four years old...The Lord was breaking down more barriers in my heart.

So, I earnestly asked the Lord for the "Gift" that He had for me, the baptism of the Holy Spirit. It is written;

"And He shall baptise you with the Holy Ghost and with fire..." (Luke 3:16b)

The Word of God means exactly what it says. I was delivering mail one day, out in a lovely rural area. It was a beautiful day, sunny and warm. Suddenly, as I was climbing back into my van, I noticed that I was becoming extremely hot. The weather hadn't changed, but my body temperature seemed to be soaring!

The first thought that I had was that I was coming down with some kind of cold or fever, but as the heat grew, I also noticed that it was an extremely pleasant feeling. It felt as if fire was coming out of every pore of my skin! When I breathed out, it seemed to intensify. I was filled with joy and peace and a sense of well- being. This lasted for about three hours. By the time I had arrived home, I understood what was happening to me and I rejoiced in the fact that God had baptised me in the Holy Ghost!

I had an overwhelming desire to preach the Word of God. The fire of the Holy Ghost had been ignited in my heart and now I prayed to the Lord that He would give me an opportunity to preach. I told my Vicar, Nicholas, who was very excited on hearing this, telling me that I was the first person to come to him in the ten years that he had been the Vicar at the church, to say that I had a calling to preach. He graciously arranged it for me to preach at The Christian Retreat (where I was born again) on a Holy Spirit day, as part of an Alpha Course. I was to give my testimony to the people in the morning, and then the course would carry on in the afternoon.

Now Rachel was in hospital at this time, due to give birth to our son, Joel, at any moment! I couldn't hang around after I had preached, I would have to leave immediately. I arrived at the Retreat, eager but nervous, to share what God had done for me. It wasn't long before Humbleman, who was leading the meeting, asked me to come up to the front to share. As soon as I opened my mouth, I knew that this was what I was called to do. The Holy Spirit filled me and the words poured forth.

After I had finished preaching, Humbleman asked the people if they had any questions for me. One lady put her hand up and they gave her a microphone. She said that she wasn't sure about God's existence but after hearing my testimony, she simply said "I want that!" meaning what had happened to me-she wanted it to happen to her.

I had to leave to go and see Rachel in the hospital, so off I rushed, without waiting to see what the Lord would do. The following week, Humbleman was telling the church what had happened on the Holy Spirit Day. He said that after I had given my testimony, a woman had stood up and said "I want that!" then he said that the Holy Spirit had fallen on the people and they had to change the entire day in order to minister to the hungry souls who were crying out for Jesus! On hearing that, I was so joyful to know that God had used me to impact someone's life for Jesus.

But what I didn't understand, because I was still young in the Lord, was that God hadn't baptised me in the Holy Ghost for merely my enjoyment alone, but rather, He was preparing me for the battle that lay ahead...

CHAPTER 4 ~ THIS MEANS WAR!

"For we wrestle not against flesh and blood, but against principalities, against powers, against the rulers of the darkness of this world, against spiritual wickedness in high places." - Ephesians 6:12

The presence of the Lord was growing in my life. After my baptism in the Holy Ghost my desire for the Lord and His Truth greatly increased. The Lord graciously guided me by His Spirit into the truth of the up and coming battle. The people of God, at the church that I was attending, would suggest other books for me to read, but I really wasn't interested in reading anything other than my Bible.

Then someone gave me a book called "Jesus, the Deliverer" by John Linden Cook. The Lord told me to read it. Now one of my first impressions of Jesus from the scriptures was that He had power! I used to believe that, if there was a God and a devil, then they would be involved in some kind of power struggle, and who knows who would win? But on reading the scriptures, I saw that Jesus had all power! In the Gospel of Mark, Jesus encounters a demon, (or a devil) in a synagogue. It started to cry out aloud, but there was no power struggle, Jesus simply told it to shut up and come out of the man in whom the demon was living, and out he came! (Mark 1:23-28)

As I read this book, I was horrified by the accounts of peoples' testimonies that were written in there. I couldn't believe that people could be so evil, but I saw that, without Christ abiding in you, people are fully set to do evil.

One of the stories was about a young girl whose parents were Satanists and they raised this girl to be a "breeder" – someone who is deliberately impregnated and then when the baby is born, it is sacrificed to satan. They made this girl pregnant, and then when she had the baby, they made her roast it and then eat it. I remember that I was moved to tears when I read this, and looking up to Rachel I said "we have to fight against this!" I didn't realize it but I had made a declaration of war to the spirit realm, and it wasn't long before the enemy unleashed his attack against me. And who did he use to attack me? My beloved wife!

Now, my friend, please understand, that my wife is the most gentle and loving woman a man could ever find. But because of sin, a demon can enter into a person and live in someone for years without anybody knowing it. Then, like with Rachel, when they want to use the person for trouble or evil, up they come and start working.

Now some Christians believe that you cannot have a demon if you are Born Again, and some believe that there are no such things as demons…I beg to differ! My wife was Born Again, washed in the Blood of The Lamb, filled with the Holy Spirit and speaking in tongues, yet she had a big boy in there! Within two weeks, my dear wife became someone whom I did not recognise. I would wake up in the night, and Rachel would not be there in bed, but sleeping outside in the back garden on the garden seat because she said that she was "infecting" us.

She became very argumentative and quick tempered. She would wake me up at two o'clock in the morning asking me to pray for her, over and over again. Her eyes would look like someone who had just been surprised- they were big and round like dinner plates. She jumped out of the top floor window because she heard a noise downstairs. She would repeat over and over, when talking about God "He doesn't love me, He's rejected me, He hates me…" She would say that, when she looked up at the stars, that they would disappear and when she looked at people, their eyes would turn into snake's eyes and they would age about fifty years in front of her. She said that when she looked at things, like a flower, that it would die.

She was so convinced that it was actually happening, that she would walk around with a video recorder to catch it on tape, so as to prove it to me. All the while I would tell her that " God loves you, He has not abandoned you, He hasn't left you" I would tell her, "Rachel, it's not real, the things that you are seeing, it is a demon that is lying to you" Praise God for His mercy, because during this period, everyone that we knew left us alone and would not have anything to do with us.

The church, where we had been born again and had been attending for two years, said "Don't come back until Rachel is healed because we don't know what to do!" The only people who really stood by us at that time were our neighbours, Peter and Karen. Karen was also struggling with depression and so they understood what we were going through. When we needed help, they were there for us, and through it, the Lord has blessed us with a wonderful friendship.

But the Lord clearly spoke to me one day. He declared "I AM going to show you that I AM all that you need." And the Lord started to show me how to fight. You know, if someone hurts their arm, it's easy to help them, stick it in a cast, and "boom!" job done! But when someone is hurt in their mind, how on earth do you help them? I mean, where do you start?

Bless the Lord for His faithful servants! My parents in the Lord, Paul and Merle were there to help. Merle gave me a book to read, "Pigs in the Parlour" by Frank Hammond, a deliverance handbook. The Lord was showing me the truth about the powers of darkness. I had seen it in Ninjitsu, I had seen it in my sister, but now it was on my front door step and there was no way that I was going to stand by and let them have my wife! The warrior that was within me started to rise up to the battle...

One day, on discovering that Rachel kept trying to run away, I had to lock the front door to keep her in, and phone for the Crisis Team- a service for people with "mental illness issues". They came and assessed Rachel in our home and recommended that she saw a psychiatrist. We were soon sat in his office, talking about all that had happened. His solution was to prescribe medicine, and he said that if Rachel refused to take them, then they would give her electric-shock therapy!

I told him boldly that Jesus would heal my wife and not his medication, to which he started to mock me. "Have you met Jesus?" he said, "As a matter of fact, I have!" I replied. "Oh! really? was that locally?" he sneered. Now I wasn't in a place at that time where I was too patient with people, my wife suffering greatly in her mind and soul, and so I wasn't too soft with this man and sternly rebuked him. There was a righteous indignation in my heart, and there still is, to anyone who would mock my precious Jesus.

It ended up with Rachel having to be committed to an asylum for while whilst they could get a better idea of what was going on in her. Now, she could only be committed to the hospital at my say so, and to give my permission was one of the hardest decisions that I've ever had to make in my life. (I wouldn't wish that upon my greatest enemy, to have to make such a decision.)

Satan had a field day in my mind, telling me all sorts of lies and filth of what would happen to my beloved wife whilst she would be in that place. He knows how to have fun with you, but praise God, my Jesus knows how to destroy the works of the evil one! I had to drive Rachel to the hospital. When we got there, there were people waiting for her, and when it became time for me to leave, Rachel begged me not to leave her there, but to take her with me and not to let her stay. It took three men to restrain her as I left the building in tears, my heart wrenched at the sight of my wife being so roughly treated, and all the while, the devil tormenting me in my mind. As I sat in the car, I lifted my voice to my God, and I knew that my wife was safe in the hands of Christ. How wonderfully does the Lord lift your burdens when you give them to Him.

After 8 days Rachel was released and was more subdued because of the medication, which helped me to be able to minister to her. She was still saying the same things, but was very subdued in her actions. She told me that she felt like she was locked up in a coffin. The doctors had diagnosed it as "Depressive Psychosis" but Dr Jesus had told me that it was a demon!

He told me to never agree with anything that demon said out of my wife's mouth, otherwise it would only strengthen its hold. So, every time it said "God doesn't love me" I would reply "That's a lie, God loves you!" (EVERY TIME! For four years!) She was still seeing the same things, nothing had changed because it was a demon, and you cannot medicate a demon out of a person. Jesus said to cast them out!

Escape Artist

During this period, I was still working as a Postman. Rachel had been keeping me up until 2 o' clock in the mornings, and I had been getting up for work at 4 o'clock. I really couldn't continue with work because I was so worn out. The people at work suggested that I should leave and be signed off work by the Doctor. I asked the Lord if that was what He wanted me to do, and He showed me that it was. So, the Doctor signed me off and I was able to minister to Rachel and try to keep the house in some sort of order. At this time satan tried other ways to bring me down.

Joseph developed a taste for running away. He thought it was great fun! Whenever you turned your back for a second, Joseph would disappear.

Once, whilst over at a sister's house, I needed to use her computer, and so I locked the front door and put the security chain on, so that Joseph, who was with me, couldn't get out, or so I thought... After a short time in the office upstairs, it struck me that Joseph was awfully quiet downstairs, and as I peeped around the door, to look down the stairs, there I saw the front door wide open! Joseph had fled!

I dashed out of the house and scanned the immediate area- no Joseph! I ran down the road- no Joseph! I carried on further until the busy main road- no Joseph! Then a couple came up to me because they could see that I was looking for something (or someone!) "Are you looking for a little boy?" they asked. "Yes, I am!" I replied, to which they answered, "We saw him cross the road, and then a car stopped, and he got in!" The devil was having a wonderful time, telling me that I'd never see him alive again! I rebuked his lies and prayed to my God for mercy. I knew that the Lord would watch over Joseph.

Suddenly, a man came up to me, "Are you looking for a little boy?" "Yes!" I exclaimed, "He's over at the Health Centre, the police have got him" and so I ran to the Health Centre which was close by. I wondered what state I would find Joseph in?

As I entered the building, there was Joseph sat on the knee of one of the officers, laughing and shouting, and the two policemen laughing with him. They hardly noticed me as I approached them, because they were having so much fun! Then one of them looked up, "Can we take him for a ride in our police car?" he said with a big smile on his face, "No! give him to me!" I said with a huge sigh of relief. The Lord had kept my son alive. It was a miracle that he had crossed such a busy road without being hurt.

A couple of days after Joseph's epic escape to freedom, my new born son, Joel, was also an object for an attack by the powers of darkness.

As I was sleeping upstairs, suddenly there was a shout from downstairs. It was Rachel. She had fallen asleep on the sofa bed whilst feeding Joel, and had woken up feeling that she had rolled over onto him. Joel was crying, and there was blood coming from his mouth, so I wasted no time in getting him into the car and racing to the hospital, which was about thirty minutes drive away.

When Joel was examined by the Doctor, he gasped when he got the results of the oxygen levels in Joel's blood... they were supposed to be 100%, but Joel's were about 55%! An X-ray showed a shadow on Joel's lungs, indicating "compression to the chest". Rachel's fears were correct! She was on medication that made her drowsy and so it was no wonder that she wasn't fully aware of what had happened. No one was to blame.

By God's grace, there was no harm done, and after a night in the hospital, they sent Joel home, perfectly well! But this showed me that I was under a constant bombardment by the enemy and that I couldn't let my guard down for one second! I was stressed and tired, but I kept my eyes on the Lord and He sustained me.

During the time that I was at home, I would go for a daily walk into the woods and fields nearby. I would be constantly declaring God's Word over Rachel's life. In the book of Romans, chapter four and verse seventeen it says that God "calls those things that are not as though they were..." and so I would be speaking out, in faith, Rachel's deliverance from this devil. I spent hour after hour building her deliverance in the Spirit, knowing that the Lord would bring it to pass because His Word says so, and I knew that He is true to His Word!

During this time the Lord had called me out of the Church of England. I had a burning desire to preach and share the Word of God on the streets, but this was not going to happen at the Church that I was attending. Also, the Lord opened my eyes to the compromise of His Word by the Anglican Church. I saw that they had wrong priorities on things.

The Lord showed me this at the annual AGM where the Church disclosed its accounts to the congregation, such as where the money that had been collected through the year had been spent, etc. Now this church that I was attending was a church in a small village. It didn't have a large congregation. The Vicar stood up and told the people that the cost for repairing the organ and bells came to a sum of about £50,000, and in the next breath he told us that they couldn't afford to hire a Youth Pastor, because they didn't have enough money!

How twisted and out of the will and heart of God it was to me! I was shocked. Added to other things that were revealed to me, and the pull of God on my heart to reach people in the streets, I knew that I couldn't stay but my Shepherd was going ahead of me to lead me in the way in which I should go, and so I followed my Lord and left that church.

The Lord united me with a couple who had a heart for street evangelism, and so I went onto the streets with them to reach the lost for Christ. They had a lot of experience with the Lord, and the Lord chose to bless me greatly by fellowshipping with them.

I started to hear of the miracles that the Lord was doing through His people, and my hunger for the real things of God grew. These people were full of testimonies of how the Lord was moving, healing and saving people through them. I wanted to be used by the Lord in the same way! I heard that white feathers were falling from the ceiling in some meetings as a sign of the Lord's presence and so, still being young in the Lord, I was impressed by such things and thought that it would be lovely to have a testimony of my own.

So, one night as I was driving to our prayer meeting, the Lord spoke to me and told me that there was going to be someone whom I would meet that night and that I was to give them my Bible as a gift. We gathered together on the common in Marlborough, for we would pray out openly and loudly on the common so that people would come to see what we were doing out of sheer curiosity. And they did come! especially the youth.

So, on this night, after sharing Christ with a self-confessed witch, she prayed to receive the Lord Jesus as her Saviour, and as she was walking off, the Lord reminded me to give her my (favourite) Bible, which she gladly accepted. I was filled with joy! As I walked away, I suddenly had a desire to look up, and as I did, a beautiful, white feather floated straight down from the sky, straight into my hand! What was strange about it, was that it was a windy night and we were out in open land and yet the feather fell in a perfectly straight line into my hand. It was witnessed by the Pastor's wife, who shouted out loud "Wow! I saw that!"

The following week, we were on the streets again and I shared Christ with an Irish lad, whose father turned out to be a Pastor. This young man was living in rebellion to his Father and he knew it, and the Lord brought conviction upon him. The Lord gave him godly advice and spoke words of comfort to him and he went away happy but convicted. As I walked away, again, I had a desire to look up, and as I did, another beautiful, white feather floated silently down and landed straight into my hand! It was such a sure sign to me that the Lord had heard my desire to have a testimony of my own and had answered me in such an obvious way! How beautiful He is.

Confrontation

One night, at the end of another prayer meeting on the common, one of the brothers that was there with me suddenly looked at me and said "be sure to be covered in the blood of Jesus when you get home!" I knew that the Lord had spoken to me through him and so I drove home with anticipation of what was waiting for me…

As I opened up the front door (which opened directly into our living room) I saw Rachel sat on the sofa. The first thing that I noticed was that her eyes were the size of dinner plates! She was glaring at me, and it seemed like she didn't blink at all. I greeted her with a cheerful "Hi!" "He doesn't love me, He's left me, He hates me!" was the immediate response that was hurled at me. I knew that that demon was up and working and Rachel had taken a back seat. "That's a lie! He loves you and He hasn't left you" was my reply for the millionth time! "Why don't you believe me? He hates me! He's left me!" was the reply, sounding like a broken record-around and around it went! I decided to go and make a cup of tea, to try and break the atmosphere, but the Lord told me that it was time…

As I was in the kitchen, rumbling around to try and make a cup of tea whilst trying to figure out what on earth I was going to do, "It" (referring to the demon not Rachel, because Rachel wasn't at home, if you know what I mean?) came out of the living room " He doesn't love me! He's left…"

Suddenly the Holy Spirit rose up inside of me, and I looked that devil straight in the eye and said "You cannot shake me anymore, my faith is too strong!" Wow, that certainly lit the blue touch paper! That devil went crazy, and grabbed me by the throat with one hand and pinned me up against the back door, whilst holding me up on my tip-toes! "What are you going to do?" I said "Are you going to punch me? It will make no difference!" I declared with a boldness that wasn't from me. The demon roared with frustration, released its grip and stormed off into the living room. I made sure that I finished making the cup of tea (like a good Englishman!) before entering the living room, hoping that the demon had "gone down."

Rachel was sat silent on the sofa, her eyes staring straight in front of her. I sat on the other end of the sofa, as far away as I could from any trouble. Suddenly "It" turned its head and, in a deep, aggressive voice, said "Why don't you believe me? He's…" "That's a lie!" I interrupted, and with that, that devil roared and jumped up and sank it's "claws" (my beloved wife's fingernails) into my arm! I jumped up from off of the sofa and declared "In Jesus' Name!" That cheeky devil just looked at me and laughed and said "Jesus…pathetic!" I was totally SHOCKED! How could a demon say such a thing?! I thought that, once I had declared "In Jesus' Name!", it would be all over! that's what I had read in so many books.

I didn't know what to do next and so I immediately stated to pray in tongues, hoping that the Lord would show me what to do. And as I did, that devil looked at me and rose up from off of the sofa and started to walk towards me like it was going in for the kill. Suddenly the Holy Spirit rose up inside of me again. I pointed straight at that devil and said "I command you to come out of her, in the Name of Jesus!" and as the word "Jesus" left my mouth, it was as if Rachel walked into a brick wall. She stopped in her tracks, then quickly walked backwards and sat down on the sofa, without saying a word, or looking where she was going. It was like watching a video in rewind! REALLY WEIRD!

I sat back down on the end of the sofa, not daring to look at her in case it provoked another attack. I didn't know what to expect next..." Oh, John! How did you get on at the prayer meeting?" It was Rachel, she spoke to me as if I had just walked in through the front door! "Err.... Yeah, it was ...err...great!" I was looking sideways out of the corner of my eyes, not quite sure what was going on. "Would you like a cup of tea?" Rachel asked. "Err... I've just made one..." I replied, still waiting for something to blow up... But it didn't, Rachel was completely set free from all "Depressive Psychosis!"

When I took her back to the Psychiatrist, he didn't know what to say. He knew that she was completely healed, and discharged her from any further consultations. He couldn't look at me in the face. The Doctors saw that Rachel was healed, and so they stopped the medication over the next few following months. Praise the Name of Jesus! There is almighty power in His Name. That's why the devil has fooled you, my friend, into blaspheming that worthy Name. You must repent and believe the Gospel! (At the time of writing, that was eleven years ago, when Rachel was set free, and she has been free ever since!) The whole warfare had lasted four years...

Now, the demon had been cast out, but it had built a stronghold in Rachel's mind, so that she was still saying the same things. The Lord started to teach me how to pray and fast, which is to go without eating food, but just to drink water, and combine it with intense prayer.

I fasted for three days, and I could see a change in Rachel in such a short time. Then the Lord told me to fast for five days, which brought more break through! Then the Lord told me to fast for seven days, in which He was speaking to me in dreams, showing me that the final victory was coming. Then the Lord challenged me to fast ten days, then twelve days, which I did, and such power was being manifested in Rachel and in the house, that the air was electric with the presence of the power of God!

Then the Lord challenged me to fast twenty one days, which, ten days into the fast, I had to stop because my body was hurting too much. This was due to a lack of wisdom on my behalf. Instead of just praying and fasting, I was busy working on the house, and so became very weak.

But the final victory came when I had the privilege to baptize Rachel in Marlborough swimming pool. It wasn't until a year later that I spoke to Rachel about that night, because I thought she might have been too embarrassed to speak about it because of her behaviour.

When I asked her about it, she said "What are you talking about?" I explained to her what had happened that night but she had no recollection at all except, she said, that she remembered me walking into the house and then feeling a huge sense of release!

Whilst reading this you might find it all a bit weird, or a bit far- fetched, but it's the truth. I was there. I saw these things (many things have not been written down for the sake of time!) I suffered through these things.

I watched my wife change from a meek, gentle, loving wife, into a raving lunatic, and then be released instantly back into her right mind, just like The Demoniac in the New Testament. It was four years of pain, struggle and torment, yet, looking back on it, it was a blessed four years because the Lord had shown me what He said that He would, and that was "He is all that I need!"

You have probably heard the saying that "Truth is stranger than fiction!" Well, it is! But these things are in the Bible, proving, once more, BY EXPERIENCE, that the Bible is the Truth. No one could help me or Rachel. The Doctors didn't have the answer, the Psychiatrists didn't have the answer, my family didn't have the answer, not even the Church had the answer.

But, my friend, JESUS IS THE ANSWER! He is the answer to all of our problems! Oh! If you would only believe in Him and trust Him, and call upon His Holy Name, then you too would see His salvation!

JESUS IS THE DELIVERER!

CHAPTER 5 ~ HAVE BAGS, WILL TRAVEL!

"And ye shall be witnesses unto Me both in Jerusalem, and in all Judea, and in Samaria, and unto the uttermost part of the earth." - Acts 1:8b

Towards the end of the fours year of battle to set Rachel free, we befriended a couple named Dave and Pam. They arrived one night at the church as we held a meeting in the Scout Hall in Marlborough. As soon as they walked in the Hall I said to myself that there was no way that I was going to have anything to do with them. Why not? You may ask.... Because they were smelly! I know that it doesn't sound very Christian of me, but when I say that they were smelly, I mean that they stank! They both had a history of mental illness, and so it wasn't their fault.

They were both dressed like homeless people, and I thoroughly judged them, and so my precious Lord was going to teach me a valuable lesson through them. On speaking to them, it turned out that they were Spiritualists- hence, the mental illness. Spiritualism, and attending the Spiritualist church will open a door for the enemy to come in and oppress you, and it was very clear in Dave and Pam's case, even though, they did have other factors in their past which would of opened up other doors. Well, that night, they both made a commitment to follow the Lord Jesus Christ, and so they joined our church.

One day, as I was going on my usual walk with the Lord in the beautiful countryside that surrounded Great Bedwyn, The Lord clearly spoke to me, "I want you to befriend David and Pamela, and I want you to be a faithful friend to them" He said. I stopped in my tracks! "Really, Lord?" I said, already knowing that there was going to be no need to protest- What thLord wants is what the Lord gets! "Yes, Lord, I'll do my best" I vowed as I cringed inwardly at the thought of spending time with Big Dave and Pam.

It was around this time that the Lord showed me that He wanted me to go back to work. Rachel was completely healed and so there was no need to spend anymore time at home on benefits, which is a humbling experience in itself! I asked the Lord what He wanted me to do, and to my surprise, He said that He wanted me to return to the building industry, not as a painter and decorator, which was my trade, but as a plumber! I had vowed that I would never work on the building sites again, but the Lord was adamant that He wanted me to learn plumbing. "Ok Lord" I said, "If You want me to be a plumber, then you'll have to give me the desire to be a Plumber, because I have no desire to be one." Over the next few days, I was filled with an OVERWHELMING desire to be a plumber... Well, The Lord provided everything I needed to take a crash-course in plumbing, He also provided the cash for a van. So, it was all systems go! I passed the course and started to advertise in my local area, which was a blessing, because there was no other plumber living in Great Bedwyn and so right from the off I was a busy man.

The Lord provided so many opportunities for me to share the Gospel with my customers. I would turn up at a job, and the customer would tell me about the problem, and I would stand there without a clue what to do! It always seemed to me that the customers knew more about plumbing than I did! But then the Lord would say "Look in such and such a place, do this, go there, this is the reason for the problem..." and somehow I would get the job done. A few times, the customers were so impressed with my work that they gave me more money than what I asked for! I was contacted by a sister in the Lord who wanted me to change all of the radiators in her house. While I was working at her house, she played a CD of a brother from Texas who was teaching on Deliverance. As I worked, I found my attention being drawn to what the Preacher (I will refer to him as "Texan") was saying, because I had experienced it first hand and it was lovely to hear that someone else had the same experiences! I asked myself why this wasn't being taught in the Churches?

The Sister gladly lent me the CDs and so I played them to my wife, who could also see that it was Truth in what he was sharing. I looked up his website and sent him an email, to testify to what he was teaching, and to encourage him to continue. His wife replied to my email and invited me to a two-week Deliverance Seminar that they were holding in Texas, USA, in two weeks' time. I knew that the Lord wanted me to go. He had set it all up, the work, the CDs, the money for me to go... there was no excuse, it was something that I had experienced and that God's people desperately needed. Rachel was in agreement.

To my surprise, Big Dave wanted to come with me, and so we prepared ourselves to travel to America, into the unknown.... I was praying that it wasn't going to turn out to be some wacky, weird seminar, where the Pastor was dressed as Elvis! After all, it was Texas....

It was the first time that I had flown in such a huge plane! The flight was to last 8 hours, and I was amazed that there was no in-flight entertainment. During the middle of the flight I needed the toilet, and as I made my way down the aisle, I saw a small group of passengers huddled together at the end of the passageway. It turned out that there was free food and snacks for passengers at the back of the plane, but not too many people knew about this… so it was lots of ice cream all the way to Houston!

On arriving at Houston, I was immediately struck by the welcome that we received, "If anyone says anything jokingly or offensive to any of the staff, they shall be immediately arrested." "Wow! America where is your sense of humour?" I thought.

Trying to get into the country proved a bit harder than I thought. The Officer was very stern when he took my passport. "Where are you staying?" he asked. "At a church, I'm here for a seminar" I replied. "And the address….?" He asked with a tone of impatience, "Oh, I don't know, someone is picking me up" I replied. "Then we have a problem!" he said. I was so tempted to say "Houston, we have a problem!" but I remembered the warning as I came off of the plane, and so I held my tongue. (It was a missed opportunity for a good laugh, but I don't think he would of appreciated it!) I walked away, not knowing really what to do, and then I saw a woman behind a desk sat at a computer." Of course, look up the address on the website!" I said to myself with a sigh of relief. I walked up to the desk and the conversation went as follows;

Me "Hi, do you think I could quickly use your computer to look up an address?"

She "What flight did you come in on?"

Me "urr…Air France…"

She "nope, sorry"

Me "Why not, you're not using it and there's nobody around"

She "I only serve Air America passengers"

Me "But there aren't any!... if you don't let me, I cannot get into the country"

She "Not my problem!"

Me "Are you kidding me?"

She – blank stare

Suddenly there appeared a man in a uniform, so I went up to him and told him the situation. He tore a strip off of the lady! I got the address and thanked the man and lined up again. As I was waiting I remembered Big Dave. I had forgotten to tell Big Dave any information- the name of the ministry, the name of the church, anything! And we had flown in on separate flights! "Oh, no! Sorry, Big Dave!" I thought to myself, as I pictured him in my head, being turned away and going back home.

Well, I managed to get through the Border and into the country. The man came and picked me up from the airport and drove me to the church where I would be staying, which was in Corpus Christi, Texas. As I walked in, who was standing there to greet me?... Big Dave! Apparently, I had given him Texan's phone number when we were back in England, and so, when he had arrived and had a problem getting into the country, he simply got the Officer to phone Texan, and all was well! There was a number of people staying at the church for the seminar, and so, the men slept upstairs and the women slept downstairs.

In the morning, Big Dave and I thought that it would be a good idea to go out for a walk and have a look around the immediate area, to see what we could see.... We ambled off down the huge highway which, eventually, led to a Naval Base. As we approached I saw the guard cross the street and make his way toward us. "Where are you two going?" he snapped, "We're just having a look around" I replied. "Show me some ID!" he commanded. Now Big Dave liked to carry a lot of stuff on him, including his Passport, whereas John likes to travel light. Oh, dear! I had no ID on me!

Now Big Dave was starting to get nervous, and when he got nervous, Big Dave would jiggle, and rock to and fro, and shuffle his feet and talk at one hundred miles an hour and start to dribble from the mouth....which he started to do! All the while I was watching the Guard's face- he was riveted on Big Dave with a "What on earth is going on with this fellow?" sort of look on his face! Then Big Dave took a step towards the Guard, who suddenly grabbed the handle of his handgun, and shouted "Stay back!" "Oh, no!" I thought "Big Dave is going to get us both shot, and it's only our first day here!" Big Dave was in full swing! with spittle flying from his mouth, whilst doing a kind of "James Brown shuffle!" All I could think of was that American's had a reputation of shooting first and asking questions later! Then I remembered to pray. "Oh, Lord! please don't let him shoot us!" was the only prayer that I could think of! Suddenly, everything calmed down... Big Dave stopped talking and dancing, the Guard released his grip on his gun and calmly said that we should leave the area immediately and remember to carry ID on us at all times. After thanking him, we did an about turn and hastily walked back to the church, all the while trying to look as calm as possible!

Now I hadn't met Texan, or seen a picture of him, I'd only heard his preaching, and had formed a picture in my mind of what he looked like- tall, slim and dressed in a business suit. Well, a man who was short, stocky (on the verge of being plump) and dressed in full cowboy gear walked into the church...It was Texan! After a short introduction, the seminar started with worship. They played a CD of a famous Tele-Evangelist who couldn't really sing, and I thought "Oh, no! not him..." as my fear of a wacky, weird seminar started to rise. THEN THE ANOINTING OF THE HOLY GHOST FELL! Wow! For the next two weeks I was immersed in the presence of the Living God...

During our stay in Texas, for some reason, Big Dave didn't want to remove his jacket, and being red in colour, it was slowly turning white with the salt from the sweat from Big Dave because it was roasting hot the entire time that we were there. One of the brothers who was staying in the church with us, approached me and asked if I could have a word with Big Dave to see if I could persuade him to have a shower, because the smell was starting to fill the entire upstairs of the church and people were starting to complain that they couldn't sleep because of it! That was Big Dave.

He had some strange ways, but the man had a heart of gold. The Lord showed me how much we judge one another by our outward appearance, whilst the Lord looks upon the heart...I was guilty of judging Big Dave once, but I came to see him as one of the best friends a man could have. I was blessed to have him as my friend.

The Lord did a great work in me whilst in Texas. I was set free from a lot of things that had been oppressing me and I received a lot of valuable teaching. The Lord confirmed that I was in His will and the two weeks were a turning point in my walk with the Lord.

Of course, the enemy didn't like it one bit! And so, after I arrived back home, he started to raise up persecution against us. Now the enemy isn't nice. He will use those who are closest to you to try to hurt you and get you off of track with God and His will for your life. It is continuous warfare. Whilst on my daily walk with the Lord, I found a lovely tree to sit under and made it a place to sit and to be quiet before the lord. One day as I was sat on a log beneath the tree, the Lord showed me a picture of a Roman Army encompassed about with shields. Then I saw that in the middle of the shields was me and my family taking shelter from the attacks of the enemy. I knew that the Lord was warning me of an attack that was coming, and sure enough, it came...

Soon after that picture that the Lord gave to me there was a knock at the door. I opened it, only to find my parents and Rachel's parents on our doorstep- a rare thing indeed! I invited them in and they sat down and quickly got to the point. They were concerned for our children, because of our beliefs, and so had contacted Social Services in order to try and get our children taken away from us and put into custody. Now, I know that their intentions were good, but they were just being used by the enemy to try to get us distracted from what the Lord had shown us. This was combined with countless abusive phone calls by members of the family.

Needless to say, the family kept far away from us. I don't have any ill feelings towards them, I only include this, not to hurt them but to show you that the enemy will use anyone and everyone he can to try and destroy your calling. They failed in their attempt! Actually, the Lord changed it into a blessing because the Social Services wrote an excellent report on how well our children were being brought up! Even, to my sadness, my old Pastor and his wife had agreed to help my family in their attempt to take our children away by telling the Social Services about Rachel's "medical history" and saying that I was forcing her to sleep in the back garden. (May the Lord not hold it against them.)

Both of my wife's parents told her that they had written her out of their wills. We were due to go on holiday together (Rachel and myself with our children, Rachel's two sisters and their husbands and children) it being all paid for by Rachel's father, but Rachel's father cancelled our tickets because he believed that it was best for all that we didn't go because we refused to agree to not talk about our Lord Jesus! We were rejoicing! It is an honour to be persecuted for the Lord's sake. That may sound strange, but the Lord fills you with such joy and peace, even in the midst of such sad and painful times. I have no bad feelings towards any of them. They were only doing what they thought best, not realising that they were but puppets in the hands of the enemy. Of course, many lies were told amongst the family about us, even spreading to our brothers and sisters in Christ, but the Lord knew the truth, and Rachel and myself were agreed and steadfast together that no one was going to stop us from doing what the Lord had called us to do- no matter what!

After a few months I was contacted by Texan. He invited me to a workshop that he was doing in Germany. I went along and saw the Lord move again with such power to deliver His people from bondage. I had never been in meetings before where the manifest presence of God was so powerful! We had agreed that England needed this teaching and ministry, and so I agreed to arrange some meetings in the Village Hall in Bedwyn. Again, we came under attack, this time from the local Vicar warning people to stay away from the meetings. Again, he was only doing what he thought was right, and so there I have no hard feelings towards him. My only regret was that there was an exchange of emails between us that wasn't, on my part, from the Spirit of Christ. (Praise God, at the time of writing this book, we have been reconciled and all is well between us.)

The meetings in Bedwyn went well, with a good attendance. Again, the Lord showed up in power and people were both healed and delivered from the power of the devil. At the end of the meetings, Texan was travelling on to Bulgaria for more meetings. He invited me to come along with him, to be part of his team, even offering to pay for my flight! Rachel agreed that I could go and so it was off to Bulgaria for the unfolding plan that the Lord had for me...

It was a very bumpy flight into Sofia, Bulgaria. The plane flew in low over the city, and the warm thermals coming up from the pollution of Sofia rattled the plane up and down. We were met by a Pastor and dear man of God, whom I will call "Praying Man" because that's what he was- a great man of prayer. Not only was he a man of prayer, but he also inspired many people to pray, especially when you were in a car and he was driving! Wow! I had never been in a car that was driven so fast and dangerously before! I saw God's protection for us, time and time again, miracle after miracle- and that was just the drive from the airport to Praying Man's house!

He lived in a wonderful house, surrounded by his garden that was full of Walnut trees, cherry trees, grape vines, chickens, and all kinds of vegetables in his vegetable patch. Bulgaria is a beautiful country- a simple and slow way of life lived in a beautiful, green and mountainous landscape with a warm and humid climate. I was in awe of the huge Pelican nests that were built on the top of the people's chimneys-they were huge! About three feet in diameter. When the mother Pelican would return to the nest, her chicks would cry for food by clacking their beaks together- it was an impressive sound to hear!

We were due to have some meetings in Sofia, then drive north to Vidin, and then back down south to Plodiv.

The meetings in Sofia went as we expected- God showing up in power and many people manifesting and being delivered from demonic power. There was a great battle in the spiritual realm as we held the meetings. As Texan began to preach, a small group of children gathered together just outside the place, who started to hammer on some corrugated sheets of metal which made a huge, distracting noise. As we resolved that problem, the interpreter, who was Praying Man, seemed to be unable to focus on what was being preached and so, he began to lose the flow of the Spirit, much to the annoyance of Texan. After Praying Man had finally settled into the flow of things, the meeting was interrupted by a huge drunken man who had heard the preaching and had staggered in from the street to see what was going on. When I say that he was huge, I mean that he was huge! He strolled up to the front of the hall and started to question and insult Texan, as he was trying to preach. People started to pray against what the enemy was doing, and eventually the man was removed from the building by at least six brothers. Thankfully there was no violence involved.

We were invited by a Gypsy Pastor to minister in his church on the Sunday. He had a church in the Gypsy shanty town that was smack bang in the middle of Sofia! As we arrived, my jaw dropped- I had never seen such dirt and filth before. People living in shacks made of corrugated iron sheets and wood. There was rubbish everywhere! the people simply emptied it into the street and the hot, humid weather made the stench overwhelming! As we walked along the rubbish strewn streets, there suddenly appeared a wedding procession! It was quite a contrast- a beautiful bride in a crisp, white bridal gown, a groom in a tuxedo and the wedding guests all dressed up dancing through the streets of filth!

When we arrived back at Praying Man's house, after the meeting, I needed to use the toilet. Now, in Bulgaria the plumbing isn't very efficient. The drains are too narrow to cope with the waste and so you do not put your used toilet paper down the toilet but in an open bin next to the toilet. So, as I was sat there, I noticed that the bin was full up to the top with used toilet paper- not very nice! So, when I had finished, like a good Englishman, I washed my hands. As I grabbed the soap, for some reason, it slipped out of my grasp and flew upwards and in a beautiful arc through the air, only to land in the poo bin! And not only did it land in the poo bin, but it managed to shuffle its way to the very bottom…I had a choice to make- I was going to be in Bulgaria for a week, the weather was hot and humid, I was sweating a lot. Was I going to leave the soap where it was and become stinky myself, or was I going to man up, roll up my sleeve and go for the lucky dip? Well, after regaining my soap, my arm literally glowed red from the scrubbing of a lifetime that it received!

Another new experience that I encountered in the Bulgarian toiletry system was the "squat over a hole in the floor" toilet. Yes, no toilet to sit on, but just a hole to squat over. This takes concentration and precise aiming, otherwise you could end up doing something in your trousers that you hadn't bargained for! But this all added to the wonderful adventure of being in an unknown country for the first time, and seeing the culture, rather than just hanging out in the "Tourist" areas.

Praying Man had acquired a mountain to pray on- yes, he had bought a mountain for 13, 000 euros. He was keen for us to see it, and so we all climbed into the VW camper van. Now it was late in the day and so he wanted us to see it whilst there was still light and so Praying Man drove extra fast (if that was at all possible!) There was, apart from me, two German brothers and a Mexican brother on board-Texan had wisely declined the invitation. The route up to the top of the mountain snaked very sharply to the left and to the right. If you have ever seen a film where someone is driving along a narrow road and there's a big drop by the road- that's how it was, and Praying Man drove up the mountain like a man on a mission! We were all praying! One of the German brothers was literally strangling the seat belt, as he clung onto it for dear life! Praying Man showed us around when we finally had reached the top. There was a few out-buildings, a lovely house and a natural spring in the back garden. And the view from the top of the mountain was amazing! It soon came time for us to descend back down the mountainside and so we all reluctantly climbed back into the van and assumed "crash positions!" About half way down the mountain, Praying Man drove the van into a pot hole that sent shudders through us all! It was only by God's grace that the front axle didn't break! We made it back to Praying Man's house alive and fully prayed up! God was certainly stretching my faith. The next day, we were due to leave for Vidin, in the north, for the next lot of meetings.

It was a beautiful sunny day as we set off for Vidin. We all climbed in the VW van, praying that Praying Man would take it easy because of the battering the van had received from the previous nights' excursion. It wasn't long before we ran into trouble! The van broke down. It had over heated because of a huge crack in the radiator-no one was surprised by this! Texan sat quietly in the front seat. He had never been late for a meeting in all the years of his ministry. We had a long way to travel, and time was running out. Praying Man was on the phone, arguing with someone whilst the Team were led out in the sun, Texan was sat praying. Suddenly two cars pulled up. In one was a mechanic, who was a friend of Praying Man. He was going to wait for his colleague to turn up with a tow-truck. In the other car was Praying Man's wife. And so Texan and I and another brother went in one car, Praying Man, his wife and the rest of the team in the other. Texan gave strict instructions to Praying Man not to drive too fast, as he didn't know where we were going, and he didn't want to get lost. "No problem!" was Praying Man's reply as he climbed into his car. Then he took off at break-neck speed! Texan was ex-Special Forces and had driven many different types of vehicles in his years of experience. It took all of his skill in driving to keep up with Praying Man as we tore through the Bulgarian countryside, going through a 50km speed limit at 150km per hour! But we did arrive at the venue fifteen minutes before Texan was due to preach! Texan quickly changed his clothes, got his Bible and walked to the front and started to preach. We could see why the enemy had tried to stop us from coming-the Lord turned up with great power and the Kingdom of God was manifested so powerfully that, as we were praying for the people, a strange noise began to fill the air. It was like a rhythmic hum that seemed to resound around the church. Later Texan said that the Lord had shown him that it was a war cry of the angels! It was an amazing thing to experience!

One thing that was strange about Vidin was that there were pictures of dead people everywhere. On houses, bus stops, lampposts there were posters of people who had died. It was a bit spooky... As we were walking along, I noticed that there were cannabis plants growing everywhere. It seemed to be everywhere you looked. When I mentioned it, a man who was travelling with us, who wasn't a believer, started to stuff as much of the cannabis into carrier bags as he could! A thought occurred to me that, if ever there was a bush fire in the city, no one would phone the Fire Brigade because they would probably be too stoned to care!

The long journey back down south to Plodiv went by without incident. Praying Man drove at a reasonable speed and it was nice to be able to sit back and watch the beautiful countryside roll past.

The church at Plodiv was pastored by Pastor Angel- a fitting name for the leader of a church! It was a thriving church, with a congregation of about one hundred people. As we prepared for one of the meetings, a couple, who had brought along their three-year old daughter, approached us and asked us to pray for her. One brother started to pray, and it was soon obvious that this little girl was demon possessed! We simply couldn't hold onto her to pray. There was four of us, but we couldn't hold her, she had great strength and moved along the floor like a snake. Every time we got hold of her, she would wriggle out of our grasp and go under the chairs! During the meeting, I started to pray for two women who were twins, whom the Lord had shown to me that they were possessed by a spirit of witchcraft that had come in through their mother. As the Holy Spirit came upon them, both of them manifested demons in the same way- their eyes rolled up so that all you could see were the whites of their eyes, and their hands and arms started to contort and become very twisted. By the end of the meeting, both of them looked like the Lord had set them free for they were both sat peacefully on their chairs. It was amazing to me to be in such meetings. Many "Church" people were manifesting demons coming out of them. People were screaming, crying, shouting, vomiting. Some were rolling around on the floor, some were being shaken by the power of the Holy Ghost as He set them free. The noise was deafening! It was nothing like the Church meetings that I had been to before, before I had travelled to Texas. The Lord was showing me the truth of many Christian's spiritual condition. Many had demons. It was the same in every meeting that I went to, whether it was in England, America, Bulgaria, Germany, Pakistan or Malaysia. It didn't matter whether the congregation believed in this or that, every time it was the same- between sixty to eighty percent of God's people manifested demons and had a great need of deliverance! And when the Holy Spirit turned up, all hell broke loose! So many were healed and set free from all kinds of sicknesses and diseases. The Lord was teaching me many things and showing me the reality of who He is and His great love for His Church.

It was always difficult for me to readjust back to "normal" living whenever I arrived home from travelling. It was such an adventure to travel with "The Team", and it was great fellowship, too. I imagined the Disciples travelling with Jesus around the land of Israel, having meetings in the open air and casting out demons and healing the sick, and here we were two thousand years later, doing the same thing! I knew that it was hard on Rachel, being left behind to cope with the house and children by herself. I knew that it was what the Lord wanted me to do at that season of my life and so it was a great struggle in my heart to go, knowing that Rachel desperately needed me to be with her, as well. I know that the Lord will reward us both for the sacrifices that we have made for the Kingdom and for the Gospel's sake. Everything must be laid upon the altar for God's glory.

Everything

The next country that we were due to have meetings in was Germany. Texan had arranged a whole bunch of meetings all around Germany, from the north to the south, from the east to the west. A certain German brother, who's wife had been healed of a major disease in one of Texan's meetings, had donated his Mercedes van for our use. He was a very wealthy man, and it was a great blessing to be travelling with all of the Team together. I flew into Frankfurt, where the first meetings were to be held. The church that the meetings were to be held in was in the middle of the Red-Light District! Next door to the church was a drug outreach centre that supplied free methadone to the local addicts. It was quite a shock as I approached the church to see people on the side of the road, with their trousers around their ankles, injecting themselves in the groin, in full view! Some were squatting down and using the side mirrors on the parked cars so that they could see to inject themselves into their necks. There was blood everywhere on the pavements. It was a real-life Sodom and Gomorrah- the perfect place for a church! Indeed, a lot of the church members were ex-addicts and prostitutes that had been won to the Lord by that ministry.

One of the members told me their story- he was a heroin addict for eighteen years. His wife had died from an overdose, but that had not changed him. Then one night, Jesus turned up in his dreams. He stood in front of this man, and then, by a wave of his arm, the floor opened up to reveal hell. Jesus said to this man, "This is where you are going if you do not stop doing drugs!" When the man woke up in the morning, he was totally free from drugs! He had no desire for drugs, and he did not go through "cold turkey" either! And when I spoke with him, I could tell that he had a real love for the Lord. We went out onto the streets together, and ministered to all the addicts and prostitutes, for they all knew him. It was a real privilege to be able to serve these people and to show them the love of Christ. The police came and told us that it was illegal to give them food and drink- just think of that... Illegal to give another human being food and a hot drink! The last I heard of that brother was that he was headed for North Korea to spread the Good News of Christ.

In one meeting, when the Holy Spirit had fallen, the people were manifesting demons coming out. There was one person that the Holy Spirit had highlighted to me, and so I went over to pray for them. As I placed my hands on them, the person was lifted up and out of their seat and flew, led horizontally in the air, backwards over about three rows of chairs! I had to try to stop them from crashing onto the ground without too much of a bump, before I could continue to pray for them. Another man, who was actually part of the Team, was showing signs that a spirit was up in him and so I started to pray for him. He fell on the ground and started to writhe around and so I jumped on top of him and continued to pray for him. We wrestled around on the floor for about twenty minutes. His legs and arms were flailing about and as he lashed out with his foot, he smashed Texan's favourite Thermos Flask that was filled with cinnamon tea that he took to every meeting. Texan was not happy...But our brother got delivered from that spirit!

We travelled to a town called Braunswag. This is the town, apparently, where Adolf Hitler was raised as a small boy. I had an overwhelming desire to preach in the streets there and so I asked one of the Team members, who was German, if he would come with me to translate, to which he agreed. We walked down the bustling shopping precinct and came to a busy T junction where people were sat outside enjoying a cup of coffee in the autumn sunshine. "Preach here", the Lord said, and so I lifted up my voice like a trumpet! The Lord empowered my voice so much, that it was so loud, and so powerful, that I thought that the shop windows would be shattered by the sound of it! It wasn't long before people became angry and came up to my face, threatening to call the police. I carried on. They tried to distract me by insults, threats of violence and asking me pointless questions...I carried on preaching. I knew that it was the enemy's way of trying to stop the Gospel from being preached. Soon I challenged the people who had been listening, that if they had any pain in their bodies, to come forward for prayer and that Jesus would heal them. Those who were brave enough to come forward were healed- every one of them! When Texan came walking up to us, he turned to the rest of the Team and said "Wow! Can you feel it?" meaning the presence of God, because the atmosphere was charged with the power of the Holy Ghost. It was such an enjoyable experience. It was always a big thrill for me to know that the Gospel had been preached, people had been healed and the devil had been put to public humiliation!

As we were driving to the next meetings, which were to be held in the north west of Germany, we decided to pull in to a Service Station for a quick break and to refuel. As we were stood on the forecourt chatting, suddenly Texan shouted "Wow! Did you see that?" "See what?" we replied, "A huge angel just went streaking through the sky, heading in that direction!" he said as he pointed in the direction of our route. "Something must have happened" he said. We all climbed back into the van and headed off down the Autobahn. It wasn't long before we hit traffic. There was a huge tail back due to a big accident that had just happened. We all looked at one another with a knowing look on our faces. Someone involved in the crash had just received some angelic help...

The Lord has taken me to Germany many times to preach and to pray for His people. I have seen so many people healed and delivered from sickness, disease and devils. I have seen the Holy Spirit move in meetings with such power, like a wave going from the front of the meeting, sweeping to the back, and then rolling back to the front, and as He moved, people would cough, shout, scream, shake and vomit out their demons. It was never a pretty sight, but then, taking out the rubbish is never a lovely job, but someone has to do it! There is still a lot of controversy that surrounds the deliverance ministry amongst Christians, but I have seen and experienced these things for myself- they are true! In one meeting, that was full of Gypsies, as the Holy Spirit started to work, one man had to be restrained by four others, in order to stop him from plucking out one of his own eyes! I 've seen respectable businessmen, doctors and people from all sorts of backgrounds behave in the most bizarre way when the power of God has been manifested. People just don't do those sort of things if demons are not real!

Trier is one of the oldest cities in Germany. It was here that Big Dave wanted me to accompany him on a shopping trip by coach. We started out from Swindon and travelled down to Dover. The ferry crossing was pleasant- the sea being quite calm, which was a huge relief to me having had some nasty experiences whilst crossing the Channel by ferry. Then, when we reached the shore, it was up through Belgium and on to Germany, where we arrived quite late at the hotel. The next day we travelled to Trier to do our shopping, and as we neared the city I saw a huge statue of Mary stood on top of a mountain overlooking to area. Immediately the Holy Spirit rose up in me with a righteous indignation, and I knew that He had something in mind... As we walked around a huge market, I noticed that there was a huge Catholic Church on the edge of the market square, and that there was, just in front of it, an empty market stall that had a platform leading up to it. The Lord said to me "I want you to preach right there!" meaning on the platform of the stall, right outside of the Catholic Church! Now I didn't know the law of Germany, whether it was legal or not to preach in a market place or outside of a church, but when the Lord says to "preach," you've got to get to it and preach!

So, I ascended the stairs and in the midst of a crowded, bustling market I lifted up my voice like a trumpet and preached against the Catholic Church and rebuked them for their idolatrous worship of Mary. Big Dave blended in with the crowd as I preached, not wanting to face any trouble, but there was only interest shown by the people, with one old man coming up to me when I had finished, to thank me for showing him the truth.

It was dinner time when we got back to the hotel. Big Dave had ordered a steak. We sat together on a long, oval table with about ten other guests. Big Dave sat opposite me, and soon I was involved in a discussion with the lady sat next to me about the Lord. Suddenly, there was a coughing noise coming from Big Dave! Now Big Dave had no table manners, as such- what you saw is what you got! Big Dave had a piece of steak stuck in his throat, and instead of rising up and going to the bathroom to deal with it, he just sat there and gagged and coughed for about five minutes! The noise was getting louder and louder with each gag and with each cough. Soon he was retching and his whole body seemed to be convulsing as Big Dave battled to strain out the blockage. Then in a crescendo of saliva and dribble the offending item was regurgitated back out onto his plate, followed by an "Ahhhhhhhrrrr!" and a stream of saliva for good measure! Big Dave just wiped his mouth on his sleeve and carried on eating the rest of his food as if nothing had happened, obviously unaware of the stunned silence, and the ten pairs of eyes that were fixed upon him in total unbelief of what they had just witnessed! I was praying for the couch to open and swallow me up…

Living for the Lord is such an adventure! He has taken me around the world to see many wonderful sights and to meet many beautiful people. He has supplied all of my needs, by His generosity. I would arrive in a country with no money and the Lord would always supply my food, and a bed to sleep in. He takes such great care of His children! I am blessed to know so many people in so many different countries. I found travelling for the Lord to be such a delight.

CHAPTER 6 ~ STREET PREACHER

"And my speech and my preaching was not with enticing words of man's wisdom, but in demonstration of the Spirit, and of power." - 1 Cor 2:4

The Lord had shown me His power to heal. The first healing miracle that the Lord had used me in was when I was working at the Post Office. I was delivering the mail on a large rural round. My boss decided that he wanted me to train another postman to do that particular round, as a back-up in case I was sick, or needed time off.

So, one morning Tony, a new postman joined me. We prepared the mail together. I noticed that his hands looked bad- the skin was very red and cracked and they were bleeding. "They have been like this for ages!" Tony said. As we drove around the countryside, I told Tony all about my wonderful Saviour.

When we got back to the office, Tony told me that he was going to go to the chemists to get some special cream for his hands. While he was gone, the Lord spoke to me. "Pray for his hands to be healed" He said. So, when Tony came back I challenged him. "Don't put any cream on your hands tonight because I'm going to pray and ask the Lord to heal them!" Tony seemed very happy when he heard that.

As I walked to the car after work, I said to the Lord "Lord, I believe that I do not have to lay hands on him to be healed, but I am going to believe like the Centurion in the Gospels and believe that You can heal him without me doing anything." Then I completely forgot all about it…

The next morning, as I was trying to wake up whilst preparing the mail, Tony came striding up to me. "Did you pray last night John?" He asked with a sense of excitement. "Errrr…no! I prayed for you on the way home, yesterday. Why?" I asked. Immediately Tony held up his hands "Look!" he said "My hands are completely healed! They have never been this good before!" he exclaimed. His skin on his hands was completely normal- no redness, no cracking and no bleeding! I was amazed. The Lord was building my faith for what He had in store for me- to invade the streets with a demonstration of His power…

After my arrival back home from Texas, the Lord gave me direction, not only to start my own ministry, but to go out onto the streets and preach the Gospel. I already had the desire, and I had been out preaching a few times over the past few years, but now the Lord wanted me to go out regularly to proclaim His Word.

I remember that after about a year of being born again, I was in Bournemouth, walking through the town centre, when I came across a man, stood in the middle of the shopping centre, boldly preaching the Gospel. I thought to myself "Lord, please don't ever ask me to preach the Gospel on the streets!" Well, after preaching on the streets now for ten years, I came to the conclusion that the Lord certainly does have a sense of humour!

The first few times that I had been out in the past, I had preached using a microphone and an amplifier. The people didn't seem to be too offended to hear me talking about Jesus. I was quite surprised by the lack of opposition that we faced back then.

After a while, with no results, no converts, no healings, no fruit, I asked the Lord why there was no opposition, or no fruit of the Kingdom being manifested as I spoke on the streets. The Lord clearly spoke to me, and what He said shocked me! He said "Because you are talking about Jesus, rather than preaching the Gospel!" This was a revelation to me! and as I prayed and pondered on it, I could see exactly what the Lord had said was true.

And so, through prayer, the Lord began to show me the message that I was to preach, a message that He had put into my heart, but a message that I had neglected by trying to preach the way I had seen others doing it.

So, armed with my microphone and amplifier, Rachel and myself, together with another brother, Christopher, who had also been coming out with us, headed to Devizes to preach The Good News. I asked the Lord where He wanted us to preach when we arrived in Devizes, and He told me to preach in the Market Place.

As we walked through the busy streets we soon came to a large open square, which we found to be the Market Place. There was a stone monument near to where we were, that I assumed to be a War Memorial of some kind. "That's where I want you to preach" said the Lord. So, we climbed the steps that led up to the monument. It was a perfect place to preach. We all knelt down to pray, and asked the Lord to bless His Word so that it would not return unto Him void. I stood up and began to preach, but this time, not telling the people about Jesus but proclaiming the Gospel.

It wasn't long before opposition came! A man came and stood at the bottom of the steps. He stood there listening, with his arms folded, for about half an hour, and then he started to heckle me, which was a good sign! He claimed to be a pagan, worshipping trees and rocks and "Mother Earth".

As I continued to preach, he soon became very angry and rushed up the steps and grabbed the microphone lead to pull it out from the amplifier. I quickly stopped him, but I was very aware to try not to do him any harm. After an exchange of words he soon calmed down and walked off and we continued on preaching. The people seemed to have become very hostile to the preaching, with many insults and threats towards us as we preached.

As we made our way back home, I thought about what had happened. I thought about what the Lord had told me. I reviewed in my mind the times when I had been out before "talking about Jesus" and now what had happened when I had "preached the Gospel". I knew that The Lord was about to show me a whole lot more! And, sure enough, I wasn't to be disappointed…

Monument of Judgement

We returned to preach in Devizes on many occasions. On one particular day, just before I was to preach, the Lord spoke to me. He said "I want you to preach on My judgement!" And so I did. I preached hard and loud.

As I did, I noticed a man and a young couple come and stand and listen to what was being said. They stayed there the whole time as I preached on the steps of the monument. After I had finished, the man approached me and said "I have brought these people here from another country, just to see this monument" "Oh, really! Why is that?" I replied. "You should read the plaque on the side of the monument" he said with a broad smile on his face.

So, I turned around and found the plaque and began to read it. It told the story of a woman named Ruth Pierce of Potterne. Apparently, she went to the market along with a couple of women to purchase some grain. They were to pool their money together in order to purchase it. The other women accused her of not giving her money into the pot, and Ruth Pierce had said that she had and that, if she was lying, may the Lord strike her dead- and immediately she fell down dead! Her money was found in her dead hand. The monument was erected to serve as a warning to others.

I was amazed! This is where the Lord had led me to preach when we first had come to Devizes, and on the day that this man had brought these people to see it, He had instructed me to preach on His judgement! The Lord was obviously speaking to that young couple, whoever they were...

Marlborough is a lovely town, boasting the widest high street in England. It was a perfect place to preach with the microphone, and so we found a convenient place, near to the Post Office so that we were sure to have a lot of people coming and going next to us.

It wasn't long, again, after I began to preach that the people were stirred up and shouts of insults and threats were hurled at us. Soon the police arrived and they threatened to confiscate our equipment if we didn't stop preaching. Well, we didn't stop preaching because we were breaking no laws, but nothing happened.

Over the ten years of preaching on the streets, I witnessed many times the police issuing empty threats. By the grace of God, I was never stopped when I was preaching, whether it was by the threats from the public, both physical and verbal, or the threats of arrest from the police- I set my forehead as flint and I carried on regardless!

The next place that the Lord led us to preach was in Newbury, the home town of my wife, Rachel. We made our way to the market square on a Sunday morning. A good time to preach, I thought-if the people will not go to church, then we will take the church to the people!

Well, my voice echoed around the square and within about ten minutes of preaching, a blurry-eyed man came shouting and swearing up to my face, complaining about the noise. He couldn't stand to hear the message of Christ. He tried to pull the lead from out of the amplifier, but, as before, I made sure that I stopped him without it leading to any form of violence. I let him blow out all of his steam, and then carried on preaching. He walked away, shoulders drooped, in defeat.

I was amazed how people were reacting to the Gospel! The same people that had not batted an eyelid when I spoke about Jesus, were now going berserk at the preaching of the Cross!

It was coming up to Christmas time, and I saw an advert for a large market to be held in Bath, right next to the Cathedral. "What a perfect time and place to preach!" I thought, and we were soon travelling to Bath with our dear, faithful brother, Christopher, coming along with us.

It was dark when we arrived, and after some trouble finding a parking space, we made our way in the cold wintry night to the market. We were greeted by lights, the hum of generators, the smell of cooked meat and, most importantly of all, lots and lots of people! The place was crowded. It was literally shoulder to shoulder, there were so many people! We made sure that we kept a careful eye on the children, who we always took out preaching with us, because we could have lost them very easily in the crowd.

We found a good place to preach, and as soon as I lifted up my voice with the microphone, security jumped on us and said that we couldn't preach at that particular spot, and so we looked for another... right outside the Cathedral! There was a little alcove on the side of the Cathedral and so we settled in there.

As we preached, it was amazing! In no time at all, the whole place emptied! I mean, one minute it was shoulder to shoulder, hundreds of people, and then the next, it was empty! The people fled from the preaching of God's Word! I had never seen anything like it before. Where they all went was a mystery, but we were probably not very popular with the stall holders, who, no doubt, suffered a huge loss of business! Bath Christmas market was turned upside down by the preaching of the Gospel. Praise God!

We also returned to Marlborough, and this time we set ourselves to preach outside of a pub that had a huge inflatable satan claws (santa claus' real identity!) over the doorway. As we were preaching it started to snow, or so we thought... the pub owners had turned on an artificial snow machine that was next to satan claws, and we were soon being bombarded by a blizzard of snow foam! Obviously, someone inside the pub had been stirred up by the Word of God and it was their feeble attempt to silence us-it didn't work!

Another favourite tactic of the enemy, whenever we preached, was for people to set off their car alarms or they would honk their horns. The devil would try anything to try and stop us, and he would use anyone to try and stop us- even members of our own families, but it never worked! God always gave us the victory.

A Bold Challenge

On another occasion, we returned to Newbury to preach. It was a bitterly cold evening. We made our way to a crossroads near the Town Centre. There was a church there, and outside of the church there was a small War Memorial that was slightly elevated above the pavement, and so, that was where we decided to preach.

After about half an hour of preaching, I started to preach against the "Theory" of Evolution. So many people stopped to either heckle me or to listen with interest that they actually blocked the road! Amongst the crowd was a group of teenagers who were particularly verbal. (It always seemed to be the young people who really wanted to know answers to the questions of life. They were the ones who usually argued the most, and I was always up for a good argument!)

These lads came up to us with their many questions. After giving them a reasonable answer to all of their questions, one of them said "Wow! I think I am starting to believe!" And so, I challenged them. "Do any of you have any pain in your body right now?" I asked. "Yes" replied one of them, "I have a broken foot! It has just had the cast taken off but it's still really painful." "Okay" I said "Watch what my Jesus can do" and I said to all of his mates "Get out your mobile phones and record this, because you are all going to see a miracle!"

Of course, they all laughed and jeered, but they started to record what was going on-obviously thinking that nothing was going to happen and expecting me to end up looking like a fool. (A fool indeed I was, but a fool for Christ!)

So, I laid my hands on this boy's foot and prayed for healing in the Name of Jesus. "Now stand on your foot and move it around" I said, which he did. "How does it feel?" I asked. He had a look of disbelief on his face " Urrr, not so painful" He mumbled. "ok, let me pray once more" I replied, and when I had, I said in a loud voice "Now run around and jump up and down and stamp your foot!" Which he did, and to his horror he was completely healed! The look on his face was one of total amazement. Then, without saying a word, he simply ran off, followed shortly by all of his mates!

As Rachel and I were talking about what had just happened, a young lad of about seventeen came over to us. He said "I have been stood over there, and I watched everything that has just happened! I want to become a Christian! "With great joy I laid my hands on him and prayed for him to follow Jesus. "Wow!" He said, "My feet feel really hot!" which was a sign to me that the Lord had done something for him because it was really was a very cold night indeed. My feet felt like ice...

When we returned again to Newbury, we started to preach in the same place, and it wasn't long before a policeman turned up! He told us that we had been reported for using "hate speech!" (It's funny how you can be accused of hate speech when you are preaching about a God of Love!) The policeman turned out to be a Christian and said that he was greatly encouraged by what we were doing and encouraged us to keep going! Praise God! He always has His people in the right place at the right time.

Chippenham was another place that we loved to go to and preach. I remember that not too long after we began preaching on the streets, that we went there one Sunday afternoon. The Lord was starting to show me how He was using the time on the streets to change me, to chisel away at all of the hardness that was in my heart, and that He was going to use the people that we met on the streets as His means to do just that!

Well, after we had prayed, we started to preach. Brother Chris and Rachel both preached loud and proud! And then, as I was preaching, a small group of teenagers gathered and started to try to cause a bit of trouble.

One of them, who seemed to be the leader, squared up to me, putting his face right into mine and saying" Are you stupid, mate, are you stupid?" I thought to myself, "Man, I could punch your head clean from off of your shoulders!... with one arm behind my back.... Whilst standing on one leg......blindfolded!" And an old friend started to rise up in me, namely, aggressive pride!

As I was entertaining the thoughts of my hard heart, the Lord suddenly spoke to me "What are you going to do, John? Are you going to punch him and so look like a hard man to them or are you going to keep your mouth shut and be humiliated for My Name's sake and look like a fool to them?" And so, I chose to look like a fool and I just stood there and took all of his insults, his taunts and his filthy language, and just kept my eyes on my precious Lord.

Afterwards the Lord greatly rewarded me by flooding my soul with such joy, that I realised it was a better way to live! not to hurt or fight back but to turn the other cheek.

On another trip to Chippenham, when we had arrived and made our way to the High Street, which was fairly busy, we started to preach. But after about half of an hour, the whole place was completely empty, and I mean, not one single person was to be seen anywhere... I couldn't believe it!

The people were like cockroaches who were caught suddenly in the light- they just had to scurry away to hide from what was being preached. The Bible says that God's Word is Light, and that men hate the light because their deeds were evil (John 3:19-21) And this is certainly true! I have seen it many times, the way people will try to avoid you when you either preach the Light or live in the Light, they just don't like it and will try to avoid you and your message at all costs.

I started to get discouraged and I thought about ending my preaching, but the Lord said "Do not stop preaching, I have people listening to you!"

And so, I continued to preach to a completely empty High Street. After we had finished, we made our way back to the car. As we turned a corner, there were three young men sat on a bench. As we passed them, one of them said "I agree with everything you've said!" And so, we stopped and turned back and spoke to them about the way of Salvation. All three of them made a commitment to the Lord in prayer, and we went on our way rejoicing! This taught me a valuable lesson, that we should not go by what we see but we should, as the Bible teaches, walk by faith and if we do then we shall see the glory of God!

Doubting Sister

The Lord also brought many people to our house for private prayer. My house was open to anyone who needed help- and there was plenty of them! One sister had invited us to dinner one night, and when the subject of demons came up, she flatly rejected the truth that a Christian could have a demon. "I simply don't believe that a Christian, who is born again, can have a demon" she said. "Well, why don't you come to my house, and I'll get you to renounce a few things, and I'll pray for you and we'll see what happens..." I replied. She agreed to this and so did her husband, who was also unsure that what I was saying was true. He agreed to come along with his wife as moral support.

We got the sister to sit on our lovely, blue sofa, and invited her to make herself comfortable and reassured her that nothing ungodly or harmful was going to happen to her. Her husband sat on a chair next to her, but not too close so as to be a distraction. I started to pray and invite the Holy Spirit to come and do a mighty work in our sister, to show her the truth of what we had been talking about, the truth of deliverance.

After I had finished praying for the Lord's blessings upon our time together, I started to lead the sister in a prayer of renouncement and repentance of her sins and of her family's generational sins that would have opened the door for the enemy to come in. We could have argued for hours about whether demons were real, or whether a Christian could have one, but all that is answered when the Holy Spirit demonstrates it clearly before your eyes! She prayed the prayer with me and then I asked her to keep her eyes open and to look into my eyes-this is because it can be quite easy to see a demon in peoples' eyes.

I wonder, my friend, how many times you have said "if looks could kill!" or you have seen someone "look daggers!" at you? It wasn't them looking at you...

I started to command the things that she had renounced to come out of her in the Name of Jesus. She just sat there and looked at me and after a few minutes, with nothing happening, she started to smile and shake her head as if to say "I told you so!" but I knew it was a ploy of the enemy to try to get me discouraged and so, give up, but I carried on.

Then the Holy Spirit gave to me a word of knowledge. "Command witchcraft to come out of her!" He said. So, I said "In the Name of Jesus Christ, I command witchcraft to come out!" and guess what happened? That demon came up in her, snarling and hissing! Her face was completely changed and contorted, her teeth were clenched together, her hands came up and her fingers were all twisted around, and that thing was right in my face, literally nose to nose, hissing, growling and trying to intimidate me! but I had run into these demons before in Bulgaria and Germany, and I knew that Jesus would get the victory!

So, I kept calm and kept commanding it to come out of her, and praise God! it came out and our sister was set free! She was slightly embarrassed though, because in the process of the deliverance, she had urinated all over our lovely sofa! But I wasn't too concerned about that. My wife and I were rejoicing with our dear sister! Her husbands chin was on the ground! He was totally shocked by what he had witnessed and said "I've never seen anything like that before! There were things in my wife's face that I've never seen before...!" They went away convinced of the truth. She came back for more prayer. She got more deliverance...

Another dear sister came for prayer. She had been tormented from hearing voices in her head, telling her to kill herself and to kill her husband. She told us that she had had them for forty- nine years! Within a few minutes of prayer, she was set free! Oh! He is a lovely Jesus! Such a wonderful Deliverer.

This woman, though, after the prayer had walked through our house urinating and defecating everywhere! Sometimes, because of the power of God, and because a demon can leave through our reproductive system, or our digestive system, people can lose their control over their bodily functions. But our house was for God's service, and so it was never an issue with us-if the people urinated, defecated or vomited (and they did!) when we prayed for them, just so long as they got free and that Jesus got the glory!

We ventured out, one day, to Bristol, to preach the Gospel and to lift up the Name of Jesus Christ on the streets. After we had parked, we made our way towards the centre of the city, but we couldn't find a suitable spot and I had a real hard time trying to find the courage to preach.

Eventually we came to an open area near to a subway, and so we decided that this was the place. But I couldn't preach, there was nothing inside of me except fear, and I couldn't seem to overcome it, which was strange, because I had preached many times before.

Anyway, Rachel took up the gauntlet and lifted up her voice for the Lord. Soon there was a number of homeless people, who had come and sat on a wall, listening to what was being said. One of them, who was drinking a can of drink, suddenly stood up and threw it at Rachel's face.

Now he was only standing about eight feet away from her, and he threw it with quite some force. It travelled through the air on a direct course for Rachel's face, who, by the way, had continued to preach.

Suddenly, the can stopped in mid- air, like it had hit an invisible barrier, and slid down right in front of Rachel's face without one drop touching her! The man who had thrown the can saw what happened and just stood there for a moment, his mouth agape! Then, without saying a word, the whole lot of them got up and made a quick exit through the subway. The

Lord knows how to deliver His people from the schemes of wicked men!

I wanted to see even more of a breakthrough on the streets. I knew that the powers of darkness were trying to keep people blind and deaf to the preaching of the Gospel.

One day, as I was in prayer, the Lord spoke into my heart and said to go and "Take the high places." After further prayer I knew that the Lord wanted me, Rachel and Christopher, to go to all of the high places that surrounded Swindon and to take Communion upon these hills and re-dedicate them to the Lord. We allowed the Lord to direct us, and He led us to some very strategic places that overlooked Swindon and the surrounding area.

After taking Communion on a few of these hills, we spotted a little copse of trees on a hill, and brother Christopher said that the Lord had highlighted it to him, and so we made our way to the top.

When we got there, we were amazed at what we found! Etched into the trees were the "All seeing eye of Horus" and tied to the trunks were pictures of dead people and their obituaries, decorated with ribbons. Then we stumbled upon a small altar that had remains of some kind of offering still upon it. We went to prayer, and we took Communion, and we kicked down the altar and rebuked the spirit of death that was in that place. It was a very eerie place to see. I believed that The Lord revealed to me that a witches' coven met there. I was in no doubt that some form of witchcraft was being performed there.

That night, as Rachel and I was laying in bed, talking about the days events, whilst my daughter and her friend was camping out in the back garden, suddenly we heard the sound of some kind of creature flying over the house. Whatever it was, it had absolutely huge wings, probably the span of the entire house because all you could hear was the slow, rhythmic "Whoosh…whoosh" of these massive wings as it flew over the roof. I didn't know whether it was angelic or demonic, but Rachel didn't waste anytime discussing it, she immediately jumped out of bed and went and opened the window and shouted "In the Name of Jesus I command you to go!" and off it flew!

I heard it, Rachel heard it and Keeleigh heard it- she was terrified by the sound of it! Whatever it was, it was either sent against us, because of what we had done in the daytime, or it was sent to protect us-I don't know but it certainly was an exciting experience and an indication to us that we were involved in some serious spiritual warfare!

Living by Faith

Now I was still working as a plumber at this time, and business was very good, actually, it was better than anything I had known before. Then one day the Lord spoke, "I want you to give up plumbing, and simply trust Me for everything you need. I will supply all of your needs, according to My Word. Go and preach My Gospel" (Philippians 4:19)

This was a big challenge to my faith- could I really trust the Lord to provide for me and my family? I decided that whatever may happen, The Lord is faithful and He would be true to His Word. So, I immediately sold my van, and contacted my customers to let them know that I wouldn't be available for business anymore.

Some of them asked me why, and when I told them, there was a hush and stillness on the other end of the phone. They thought that I had gone crazy and so did my family and members of the Church! I had a wife, four children and a mortgage to support without any income. But the Lord is true to His Word, and it wasn't long before people began to support my ministry.

I didn't ask anyone for money, but people would phone me up and tell me that the Lord had placed it in their hearts to give a donation or a regular gift to support the work. On a few occasions, after preaching on the streets, complete strangers came up to me and gave me money!

The Lord showed to me His faithfulness to provide for me and my family, time and time again. One night, as I was walking up the stairs to bed, I turned and said to Rachel "Please remind me tomorrow to get some lightbulbs." Our house was in virtual darkness because most of the lightbulbs that we had had blown. We had many different kinds of lightbulbs, as well! Spot-lights, bayonet fittings and screw-in fittings, all of different sizes.

The next day we spent taking our children out to the beach. I had completely forgotten about the lightbulbs, and so had Rachel because she didn't remind me to get any more new ones. On returning from our day out, I pulled up onto the driveway and parked the car. I opened up the porch door, and to my amazement, tied to the handle of my front door was a carrier bag... a carrier bag full of lightbulbs! And not only full of lightbulbs, but of every type and size that I needed!

You don't need to tell me that God provides for all of our needs- I know that He does!

This, obviously, gave me a lot of time to seek the Lord. I was very excited, because I had a lot of people coming to my weekly meetings, I had people coming to my house for regular prayer for issues in their lives that they wanted deliverance from and I had invitations to preach in other ministries.

So, I was expecting for it to get even busier but within about a month of stepping out in faith and trusting the Lord, everything seemed to dry up! People stopped coming to the meetings. People stopped coming for prayer. I couldn't understand it and so I sought the Lord to reveal to me what was going on.

He clearly spoke to me "I want you to seek Me, first and foremost" He said "I will bring the work along in time, but first spend time with Me, and when the times comes, you will be about My business." With that, I trusted the Lord and so spent most of each day walking in the beautiful countryside that surrounded Great Bedwyn, talking and listening to the Lord.

It was a wonderful time of revelation and abiding in His wonderful presence! I was so blessed to spend time reading His Word and meditating upon it in the fields. I grew very close to the Lord. Obviously, the enemy didn't like it and tried many ways to distract me, but The Lord was very gracious to me and always enabled me to spend precious time with Him.

Now one day, as I was out walking with my Lord, He said "I want you to move to Swindon and preach the Gospel." Now, we had been going to Swindon every Sunday afternoon to preach, and we had experienced a lot of opposition, especially from the shop owners who regularly called the police, claiming that we were affecting their business! Also, when Rachel and I had left Newbury, to live in Bedwyn, I had sworn that I would never live in a town or city again. It was with reluctance that I said "Yes Lord" not really meaning it in my heart, for I loved living in Great Bedwyn and I didn't relish the idea of living in Swindon. But, in obedience, I put the house on the market and waited to see what would happen.

Nothing did happen.

No one was interested in buying our house. After about a year I asked the

Lord what was going on. Had I misheard the Lord? But the Lord showed me that my heart was not willing to move and so, there would be no move to Swindon until my heart was truly willing…Well it took three years! But there came a day, again, that I was out walking with the Lord, and He asked me again "Will you now move to Swindon?" "Yes, Lord, I will" was my reply from my heart and so I put the house on the market once again. It went live online for sale on a Thursday evening at midnight, and the next day, by 11 am it was sold for the full asking price! (Much to the amazement of the Estate Agent!)

When I had said "Yes" to the Lord about moving to Swindon, I did lay down a few conditions…I wanted to sell my house and then be able to buy a house, in Swindon, outright, so that I didn't have a mortgage anymore. Also, I wanted a four-bedroom house, with some out-buildings, reasonable sized gardens and my wife wanted a pantry in the kitchen. Well, after we sold our house and paid off the mortgage, we were left with £120,000.

We found a house in Swindon, that as soon as I walked into the hallway, I knew it was the one! It had four bedrooms, an outside toilet and workshop, large gardens and a pantry in the kitchen! And the price? £120,000! The Lord is so good and gracious.

It wasn't long before we had gone through the trials of moving house, and were soon settling into our new house and facing a new season in our walk with God!

A Sign to Swindon

The Lord said to me "I want you to preach the Gospel and confront the people of Swindon with My Son, Jesus Christ. I want them to hear about Him. I want you to get in their face! (That's how He put it.) You will be a sign to the people of Swindon, a sign that shall be spoken against…"

It was very exciting for me to be able to preach full time on the streets of Swindon. The word "Swindon" means "Pig Hill" and it certainly has a reputation for being a rough town. Like most towns, Swindon suffers from gang violence and from drugs. Prostitution is also a big problem for this town.

But what the Lord had taught me with Big Dave, in that I shouldn't judge people by their appearance or by their reputation, He also showed me in Swindon and gave me the privilege to get to know many of the gang members, druggies and prostitutes – people that I would have never, ever had associated with if I had not gone into the streets to preach!

Now don't get me wrong, it wasn't as if I was loved or even liked by them. Actually, many of them hated me but the Lord put a great love in my heart for them all. My preaching was very strong and uncompromising. The Lord gave me a mighty anointing to preach.

I would make my way into town- a walk of about forty minutes, and all the way I would be thinking about what may happen to me if I said this or that. The enemy would play havoc with my mind. I would walk into the town centre in fear and trembling but as soon as I opened my mouth, the Lord would give me such a boldness, that I knew that it didn't come from me! I would preach fearlessly and the whole town would be stirred up by the preaching!

So many times the police were called or Security was called by the public to try and stop me. They tried everything they could- physical violence, verbal abuse, threats of being arrested, threats of being thrown through the shop windows, threats by a man convicted of firearms offenses, that he was going to shoot me if I didn't stop.

I had everything you can think of thrown at me- water bombs, fruit, vegetables, raw eggs, snow balls, sweets, coins, a man picked up his bike to throw at me, I had a Sodomite (The Biblical name for a Homosexual) baptize me with his bottle of Coke, I was spat at.

They would spit at me as I walked into the town, before I had even spoken one word! They would spit in my Gospel tracts and then throw them back at me, or they would set them on fire. I was accused of saying all sorts of terrible things that I never said. I was known by the police and was on first name terms with them!

On social media, pages were closed down because of the threats of violence and the foul language that was used against me. I received hoax phone calls with people mocking my wife and me down the phone. I would be out in all weathers, snow, frost, hail, wind, rain, sunshine, whatever the weather, I was in town lifting up my voice for my lovely Jesus, the One Who died for me! But through all of this, my heart would be all aglow with love for them! And there was much, much more, and all because I told them about the Gospel of God's Grace and Love!

The Apostle John wrote, "Marvel not, my brethren, if the world hate you..." and how true these words are! (1 John 3:13)

Jesus said "I have chosen you out of the world, therefore the world hateth you." (John 15:19b)

I have mentioned before how that I was frustrated with the lack of fruit when I was "telling the people about Jesus," rather than preaching the Gospel. The same happened regarding praying for people to be healed on the streets. Now, I had seen some people healed, but I believed that I should be seeing more people healed and so I took it to the Lord. Again, I was surprised by what He said, "The reason you are not seeing people healed is because YOU are trying to heal them!" He said "It is My Name that is at stake, not yours. It is My Gospel that I will confirm with signs and wonders. It is My power that will heal them, not yours. You cannot heal anyone."

He continued. "The reason that you get so frustrated and disappointed is because you preach to see people saved, you preach to see people healed, you preach to see people delivered..." "But isn't that what I'm supposed to do, Lord" I said. "Yes, but if your PRIMARY reason for preaching are these things, then you will always be disappointed if these things do not happen. Let your PRIMARY reason for preaching the Gospel be for MY GLORY, and then, no matter what happens, you will never be disappointed." This was such a beautiful revelation that set me free from me trying to do it all by my wisdom and strength to make things happen! So, armed with this knowledge that,

I cannot heal anyone, but Jesus can and will if I preach His Gospel!

Preach for the Glory of God alone and leave the results up to Him!

I made my way onto the streets excited and expectant of what was going to happen. And, boy! I wasn't disappointed...

Rachel, Christopher and myself, with a new brother that started to join us on the streets, all made our way into the heart of Swindon's town centre to declare the truth of the Gospel. We started to preach in a large open square where many people gathered.

There was a gang of teenagers sitting on a wall that started to throw stones at us whilst we preached and so I went over to them to confront them with Christ! Of course, as I started to speak to them they just mocked and ridiculed my faith and confessed that they believed in Evolution, even though, when challenged, none of them actually knew what Evolution was! (Unfortunately, like so many others, they had been indoctrinated rather than educated by the Education system.)

So to cut across all of their objections I asked if any of them had any pain in their bodies, telling them that Jesus was real, that He is alive, and that He is not a dead religion! They all went very quiet, and looked a bit unsure of what to say. They didn't know how to react to such a direct challenge- they were okay with questions that they could answer and refute or mock but this was a new thing for them...

Then one of them, a young girl, said that she had pain in her feet because she was flat-footed. I said boldly to her "Put your feet into my hands, and Jesus will heal you!"

As I knelt down on the ground in front of her, I repeated the challenge. "Come on!" I said "Put them into my hands and Jesus will heal you, just have faith!" She looked around at her friends, who were all jeering and laughing, and then she slowly put them into my outstretched hands. Instantly she gasped! "Something's happening! They feel really weird!" She exclaimed, much to the amazement of her friends! Then she suddenly jumped up and started to rock backwards and forwards on her feet. "They feel different" she said "I feel really light on my feet!" "I 've never felt like this before!" The Lord had grown arches in her feet and had healed her of being flat-footed.

When the others saw it, they were amazed! Then one of them said "I have a headache, could you pray for me?" "Yes, of course!" I said, and when I did she was instantly healed! Then another one of them asked me to pray for his eyesight, which I did, and to his amazement, he said that he could see better!

Again, another one asked for me to pray for her painful knee, which, when I laid my hands on her, Jesus completely healed her! Another came up to me and said "Could you give me some money to get a drink?" I handed him a twenty-pound note and told him to keep the change! His chin hit the floor! They were all amazed and could not speak against the Lord after this because they all experienced His power and so they went away joyful! (Whenever I saw them again, they were all very friendly and never again mocked the Lord!)

I walked away with so much joy in my heart. Jesus had turned up and confirmed the message of the Gospel with signs, wonders and miracles, just as He said that He would do in the Holy Scriptures!

As I sat down on a bench to talk with Rachel about what had just happened, Peter, the disciple who had started to come out with us, came up to me laughing and said "You must of got soaked!" "What do you mean?" I asked. "Well, I was sat over there watching you, and when they poured that bucket of water over that girl that you first prayed for, you must of got soaked!" he replied with laughter in his voice. "What are you talking about? There was no water" I said, feeling a bit confused because Peter was so definite about what he had seen.

He was adamant that he saw a huge amount of water being poured over the girl as I prayed for her, and so to settle it, I took him over to the place and showed him that the area was completely dry on the ground, there was no sign of any water anywhere! He was much perplexed by this! I explained to him that he must have had his spiritual eyes opened at that moment to see the Holy Spirit, Who is compared to water in the Scriptures, falling upon that young girl as she was healed! We were all very excited about this because, again, it was evidence to us that the Lord was with us and that He was starting to move in great power on the streets of Swindon…

Highs and Lows

The following week we all met up again and decided to preach a bit further down the High Street, but afterwards we would make our way back to the open square to give out Gospel tracts and talk with the people.

As we were handing out the tracts, another gang of teenagers came up to us and started to mock and swear and just generally be obnoxious. And so, I challenged them as I challenged the other teenagers the week before. "If any of you have any pain in your bodies, let me pray for you. The Lord Jesus will heal you to show you that what I am saying to you is the truth!"

Again, they were not used to being challenged in this way and so they were slightly unsure as how to answer. Then one young girl said "I have a painful left knee" "On a scale of one to ten, ten being the most painful, what number would it be?" I asked. "Definitely an eight!" she said without any hesitation. "Okay, well if you let me pray for you, Jesus will heal you" I confidently affirmed. "Okay!" she replied, and when I laid my hands on her and prayed a very short prayer, I told her to walk around to see how it was. "There's no pain!" she exclaimed "It's totally gone" she said and then quickly turned to her friend, who was sat on his bike watching what was going on, and said "Let him pray for you, and you shall be healed as well!" (I was amazed at this, because in doing so, she expressed more faith for healing than most Christians I know…)

He had broken his knuckles in a fight the night before, but he was willing to let me pray, and when I did- Jesus healed him! To which he testified that there was no longer any pain in his hand! He grinned from ear to ear and turned around and rode off down the street on his bike without saying another word! (I could understand this because he was publicly mocking the Lord, and then when he was healed, there was nothing he could say against it but he had to eat some humble pie!)

Again, all the members of that gang wanted prayer for various ailments, and all testified of being healed, much to their amazement (and, to be honest, much to my amazement too!) It seemed like the Lord had broken out on every side, and anyone who wanted prayer, "Boom!" Jesus healed them, just because He can! He is so lovely!

That young girl had encountered the Lord in a real way. Her face was lit up with joy. From that time on, for the next two years or so, every time that I saw her on the streets, she would shout and wave, and I was always sure to tell her that Jesus loved her. She even added me as her friend on Facebook! (As did a number of the youth that we had prayed for did.) I would look on her updates to see if there was any change in her way of life, or any confession of faith in Jesus. There didn't seem to be…

She was killed in a car crash at the age of eighteen.

You know, my friend, it's not an easy life following Jesus. Through preaching the Gospel on the streets, The Lord had put so much love into my heart for the unlovable. For the outcasts. For the gang members. For the prostitutes. For the drug addicts.

I told them about the Lord, how He could really make them free from their burdens of sorrow and pain. My heart yearned for them to know His goodness. He could change their whole situation. But they rejected Him and stayed in their pain. Time after time after time, I had pleaded with them.

The Lord had shown them His power, and yet, they went on in their stubborn rebellion. Could your heart bear that? Being rejected time after time, when your heart is bursting with love and compassion for them? Seeing them die? Being spat at. Being cursed and swore at. Being threatened day in, day out. Being mocked because you care for them and are willing to be humiliated for their sakes. Could you carry on loving them? One day they were on the streets, and then the next day I would hear that they had overdosed, or some other terrible thing had happened to them.

Then you have to suffer all of the backlash from the people when you continue to preach about a God of love. It's no wonder that, in the Scriptures, Jesus is described as "A man of sorrows and acquainted with grief" (Isaiah 53:3) The Lord was allowing me to share His burden for the people, and Oh! how it crushed my heart and broke it into a thousand pieces!

Then I would have my, so-called, brothers and sisters in Christ, come up to me whilst I was preaching and publicly rebuke me for what I was doing! This was one of the most surprising things to me when I started to preach in the streets. I expected to be insulted and rejected by unbelievers, because they know no better, but when a brother or sister in the Lord comes up to you and starts to rebuke you in front of unbelievers for preaching the Gospel to them, it was a huge shock to me!

But eventually, I got used to it, and after a while, anyone who came up to me to rebuke me had to be prepared to be publicly challenged by myself as to why they professed to love Jesus, and yet hated His Word! This was a typical conversation with a brother or sister who took offense to what I was doing...

Christian : "You shouldn't be doing this, you're doing it all wrong"

Me : "Doing what wrong, exactly?"

Christian: "Preaching! You're doing it wrong. You should be telling them about the love of God!"

Me: "Oh, I see! So how do you preach to them about the love of God? Could you show me?"

Christian: "I don't"

Me : " I'm sorry, did you say that you don't tell them about God's love?"

Christian "No, and what you're doing is wrong!"

Me : "Do you believe that the Bible is true?"

Christian : "Yes, of course I do!"

Me : "So are these unbelievers going to hell?"

Christian : "Urrrrr….well…ummmm…" (Never , ever, do they answer that question…)

Me : "So you're telling me, that by telling them to repent and believe in Jesus, so that they do not perish in hell, is wrong and that I should stop, and yet you say that you believe that the Bible is true, and yet you do not warn them yourself about hell… Well, could you please go away from me because you are nothing more than a religious hypocrite!"

And generally things would go from bad to worse from that point onwards…I didn't make many friends amongst the religious Christian community!

To be honest, I found that over the years, the worst opposition didn't come from the unbelievers, but from those who apparently "confessed" Christ! This is a sad statement for me to make, but I have seen it and lived it by experience and have had the above conversation many times on the streets. It was a huge grief to my heart. I simply cannot understand how a Christian would not want another Christian to share the Gospel with the lost, whether they judge you to be doing it right or wrong. And to tell you to stop preaching the Gospel, when they themselves do not preach…

We will all have to give an account of what we have said and done before the Throne of God.

During my time on the streets I got to know a lot of the people who sold "The Big Issue"- a magazine that helped the people who were selling them, who were usually homeless or poor, to obtain some kind of income.

A Wee Scot Named Tom

One of these was a small Scottish man named Tom. I would always make a point of speaking to Tom, to make sure that he knew that he was noticed by someone. So many people walk past them as if they don't exist.

One day I was in the Town, standing upon a small wall that had become a regular spot for me to preach, when Tom came walking up to me. Accompanying Tom was Kevin, a drug addict and drunkard who always insulted me and shouted at me whenever he walked past as I preached. I had known Kevin for about four years. He had asked me, about two years before, to pray for him because he was going into prison and he wanted to straighten out his life. These people may ridicule you and abuse you, but they know who to come to when they want help!

So, Tom and Kevin came walking up to me, and Tom asked "John, do you have a tenner that you could give to me so that I can get a bed for the night?" "I'm sorry mate" I replied "I don't have any cash on me". Then the Lord spoke to me "What about your debit card?" "Sorry, Lord. What did you say?" I replied. "John" The Lord said "I want you to show this man that there is someone who trusts him. I want you to give him your debit card, tell him your PIN number and let him go to the bank and draw out however much money he needs!"

I was shocked at this, but I quickly got myself together and I said to Tom "Here is my debit card, this is my PIN number, go and take out of my account whatever amount you need. I trust you" There was a silence…Tom looked bewildered. Tom looked at Kevin. Kevin looked at Tom. Then Tom hesitantly took my card and off he went. I carried on preaching.

About ten minutes later Tom returned and handed me my card. "Look!" he said, holding out a ten- pound note "I have only taken out a tenner" he said. "Yes mate" I said, "I trusted that you would." Well Tom went off to get his room for the night as a very happy Scotsman!

About a year later I was preaching in the same spot when who came walking up to me but Kevin. This is how the conversation went…

Me : " Hi Kevin, I haven't seen you for a while. How are you doing?"

Kevin : "John, I am a Christian. I read the Bible. I go to church. I have a lovely woman and have taken on her children as my own. I have been clean for a whole year. I haven't drank or taken any drugs whatsoever! I am completely clean!"

Me : "Wow Kevin! Praise God! That is wonderful news!"

Kevin : "Yes! And it's all because of what I saw you do to Tom last year. John, I've never seen anything like that before! I had heard you preach for years, and never believed it, but when I saw you give your card to Tom and tell him to go and take out whatever amount that he wanted from your account…well…I just couldn't believe it!"

I was so humbled by what I had heard that I couldn't continue to preach that day. I walked home with tears in my eyes. I was in awe of God's goodness. This precious soul had been reached by God's love, by a foolish man on the streets, willing to take risks for His Lord's Name sake. A soul saved from an eternal judgement. A soul saved from Hell. And Christians would still be coming up to me, telling me that what I was doing wrong. May the Lord forgive them and not hold it to their account.

During the "Festive Season" we would always be excited about the crowds that would be in the streets!

One day, just as the light had faded, and so all of the streets were lit up with the beautiful lights, we were out preaching and giving out Gospel tracts. (We always had people coming up to us and saying that no one was interested, and yet over a three-year period, we gave out around 60,000 Gospel tracts in Swindon, alone!) A gang of young people had stopped and were listening to us.

After we had finished preaching, I started talking to one young man who confessed to be a Catholic. I told him the Gospel and why he should renounce the Catholic faith. "My friend," I said "Jesus is alive and He wants you to follow Him!" At hearing this faith seemed to rise up in him. I asked him "Do you have any pain in your body?" "Yes," he replied "I have a very painful back- I've always had it!" he confessed.

I turned to the crowded street, knowing what my Lord wanted to do. I shouted out as loud as I could "If there is anyone who doesn't believe in God and wants to see a miracle, come here, because Jesus is going to heal this young man!" This drew quite a crowd. I then challenged them to get their phones out and record what they were about to witness!

I sat the young man down and measured his legs, and sure enough, one leg was longer than the other. I explained this to the crowd and the young man in a loud voice the reason for his pain. He confessed that, on a scale of one to ten, the pain was a ten plus! I said a simple prayer, and his leg grew out to the same length as the other! He stood up in amazement! "What shall I do?" he said "Shall I run down the street?" "Yes, of course!" I replied, to which, on hearing this, he immediately sprinted down the street and around the corner and disappeared!

I was hoping that he would return…

About two minutes later, he came sprinting back from around the corner and back to his waiting audience. "I'm healed! I'm healed! There's no more pain!" he shouted out. I turned to the crowd and proceeded to preach the Gospel, to a now captive audience.

Angry Paul

Paul was a big man. Paul didn't like us preaching the Gospel. The first time I saw Paul was when he was verbally abusing my wife because she refused to focus on the issue of Joseph having Down's Syndrome-something that Paul had taken an immense dislike to!

I was preaching by myself, one day, in the High Street when a drunken Paul came staggering up to me. As I preached, he started to shout in my face, literally pushing his nose into mine. His faced was cherry red and his breath stank of beer. He was very aggressive, and started to push and shove me around. I kept on preaching and completely ignored him. After a while he staggered off and I, feeling very relieved, carried on preaching, still in one piece!

When I had finished, I started to walk down the street, but was met by an angry Paul. "I hate you!" he said "If there were no people around I would give you a good hiding!" "I'd love to drag you to a car park somewhere and give you a good beating" he said. "My friend" I replied, with absolutely no fear in my heart because I knew that God was with me, "The Lord can take all of your anger and pain, and all of that violence from out of your heart. He did it for me and He can do it for you!" Paul was completely taken back by the tone of my voice and what I had said to him. He was expecting me to retaliate in anger or with threats, but the Lord just flooded my heart with love for him. He walked off without saying another word.

I started to preach again in another area of the town centre, when I spied Paul, leaning against a shop window, listening to every word that I was saying. As I walked home, the Lord said to me" Whenever you see Paul, I want you to shout out to him and make sure he hears you. Be loving towards him." So, every time that I saw Paul, I would shout out "Hey, sir! How are you today? It's good to see you my friend!"

About a few months later I was sat on a bench, preparing myself to preach, when Paul came walking up to me. He said "Mate, I'm so sorry for the way that I treated you a while ago. I just cannot understand your message. I've tried to but…" Then he went on to tell me that his Mother had become a Born- Again believer, who was a strict Buddhist in the past, and he couldn't understand what had happened.

He told me that he desperately wanted to believe, to encounter God in a real way. He seemed to be very frustrated. I was amazed by what he said and by the change in his attitude towards me. He was now very meek and polite and friendly. We became good friends and often had some lovely conversations on the street. I prayed for him to know the Lord...

Troubled Tyler

Tyler was a young man in his early twenties who was out on the streets one day collecting money for children with cancer. I was preaching in an empty shop doorway in the High street. It was one of my favourite places to preach. I was accompanied by a brother who had flown from Germany so that he could come out and learn how to preach the Gospel on the streets. Over the years I had many people come from Germany to come out onto the streets, so that they could learn how to preach the Gospel and to see the wonderful miracles of healing that the Lord was doing in Swindon.

Tyler walked up to me and said "Excuse me mate, you wouldn't mind moving down the street and preaching would you? Only no one is giving money because they're distracted by you!" "No sorry mate, I'm going to carry on preaching right here!" I replied, because I knew it was where the Lord wanted me to preach. "Come on mate, be fair" He said "I'm trying to collect money for children with cancer" "Mate" I replied "I know a God Who heals cancer! But even if the children are healed of cancer, they will still die in their sins without Christ!" I said.

Tyler exploded!

He threw a punch that glanced off of my head, knocking my hat off and onto the ground. I took no notice, but simply looked for my hat, picked it up, put it on and carried on preaching. All the while Tyler was shouting and swearing and threatening me. The guy was hysterical! He stormed off, very upset, but I knew that the Lord had "pressed his buttons." The Lord was trying to reach him.

I eventually finished preaching, and so me and the German brother decided to go and get a hot drink. As we turned the corner, there was Tyler walking towards me. As soon as he saw me, he spat at me and started to swear. I simply blessed him and carried on walking. I knew that the Lord had stirred something up in him.

After our drink, we made our way back through the street to head for home. I saw Tyler stood to near where I had preached. The Lord spoke to me "Go and give him that five pound note that you have in your wallet. Do not say anything to him". "Yes Lord" I said, desiring to be obedient. Tyler had his back to me as I approached him, but as soon as I was near he suddenly turned around. I put the five- pound note into his pot, turned around and walked away without saying a word. I prayed for the Lord to move in Tyler's heart and for the Lord to heal his son.

About two months later, I was preaching in the same place when a young man approached me. He introduced himself as "Tyler" and proceeded to apologize for his behaviour towards me. He explained that at that time, his son was suspected to have developed cancer and he was very upset and then when he heard what I said, he had simply lost control! We talked and I explained to him the Gospel and he said "You know, what you're doing out here is such a good thing! I thank God for what you're doing!" he said. The Lord had changed his heart completely! His son was completely well. They had misdiagnosed him...

The large open square became a favourite place for us to evangelize one-on-one. We would preach the Gospel in the busy shopping centre and then walk down to the square where the people came to sit on the benches so that they could watch the huge public TV screen that dominated the area.

The Lord told me to go over to a bench where three young women were sat. They were engaged in a conversation when I walked up to them and offered each one of them a Gospel Tract. This allowed an opportunity for me to ask them about their beliefs, and of course, when they denied the existence of God, I challenged them to allow me to pray for them.

As usual, I asked them if they had any pain in their bodies. One of the young women, who was sat in the middle, told me that she had a very painful back, which she had suffered with for years. The Lord directed me to measure her legs, to see if they were the same length, which I did by getting her to sit with her back pressed up against the back of the seat, and for her to place her feet into my hands.

One of her legs was clearly shorter than the other by about half an inch. I explained to her that this would be the reason for the pain in her back because her whole structure would be misaligned due to the short leg. "If you let me pray for you, Jesus will heal you to show you His love for you, and that He is alive and that all that I have told you (The Gospel) is the truth". "Okay!" she replied. And so, I held her feet in my hands, and I asked her two friends to carefully watch. They could see that there was quite a difference in the length of her legs.

I prayed a short pray and just before I had finished praying the young woman's leg shot out to the same length as the other one! The woman gasped, and her two friends were actually physically shaking from shock at what they had just seen! I told her to stand up and to prove that she had been healed I asked her to do whatever it was that she couldn't do before, to which, she responded by bending over and touching her toes. "I have never been able to do that!" she exclaimed with a beaming smile. Her two friends confirmed it.

She walked away pain free and amazed at having an encounter with the Living God! A few weeks later, I was in the same place when this young woman came walking out of a fast food restaurant. I asked her how she was and she confessed to being absolutely healed of all of her past back problems!

We have such a Lovely Jesus!

Peter the Puncher

At this time there was a spate of riots that were spreading from city to city because of an "injustice" that had been done to a young black man in London by the police. I don't remember the full details of the story regarding the conditions that ignited the rioting, but I do remember that in city after city, there were riots and the people were looting the shops.

There was a rumour on the streets that a large number of people were coming in from Bristol, and other cities that had rioted, by train, and that a riot was going to break out in Swindon. "What a great opportunity to preach the Gospel to the crowds that would be gathered!" I said to my wife and to our brother Christopher. We all agreed that it would be a wonderful time to preach and so we made our way down to the town. It was fairly dark and late on a Wednesday evening when we got into town.

We were not disappointed…there was a huge crowd of people that had gathered in the centre, and a large number of police, too, even some on horseback! Obviously, they were expecting trouble. We were soon on our knees, in front of them all, praying to the Lord, that He would spare Swindon from rioting. Well, we were soon preaching, and it wasn't long before the people started to get stirred up, much to the concern of the police, who tried to get us to stop. But the preaching actually took the people's attention from off of rioting, and they were refocused to listening and heckling the preaching of the Gospel!

I started a conversation with a man named Peter, who was in the area because he was due to take part in an illegal bare-knuckle fist fight that night. Peter was a prize fighter. He was a big, tough man. His face was scarred. His eyebrows were swollen. His nose had been broken more than once. He had cauliflower ears. But the most obvious sign was that his right hand was paralysed into a semi- clenched fist. He told me that because it had been broken so many times through punching people, that he had lost the ability to open and close it.

He was busy preparing for the fight by getting drunk on cider as I told him about the love of God. He was very open to the Gospel. He kept asking me "Am I gonna win tonight, John? Am I gonna win?" I said "Peter, win or lose, I pray that God will take that fight from out of your heart, and that you would know His peace." I asked him if I could pray for his hand. "Of course!" he said. I held his hand and prayed...then I grabbed his fingers and started to straighten them in the Name of Jesus! The Lord completely healed his paralysed hand!

Peter was too drunk and too distracted by the up- and- coming fight to really notice. When he shook my hand as we parted, it was with a fully working hand! There were no riots that night, or any other nights following, in Swindon...

I continued to pray for Peter. The Lord had given me a love for him. I would often wonder what might of become of him.

Because the Lord is so gracious, about a year later I was walking through the high street after preaching. I instantly recognised that beaten up face sat on a bench- it was Peter! I went up to him and said "Hello". We got talking. He told me that he couldn't remember much about that night...but for a whole year, since that night, he had not drunken any alcohol, and that he had given up Bare Knuckle Fist Fighting! He was no longer a prize fighter! I remembered the words that The Lord had given me to say to Peter, and the Lord had done the work in his heart-the fight had been taken out!

By the way, he had greeted me with a perfect right hand shake! His hand was still completely healed!!

On another occasion, as I was preaching in a crossroads in the town centre, a young woman came hobbling past on crutches. The Lord suddenly spoke to me "pray for her!" He said, and so, I called to her "Madam! if you let me pray for you, Jesus will heal you because He loves you!" She came over to me. "Will you let me pray for you?" I asked "Sure!" she said "But you can't touch me!" she protested. "Okay, that's no problem for my God!" I said and immediately started to pray.

Then I asked her to feel if her leg had been healed. She said that the pain had reduced, but there was still some pain there. So, I said "Let me pray one more time!" and so, after another quick prayer, I just grabbed the crutches from her and in a loud voice said "Now run around!"

The young woman had faith, because she did! and then exclaimed "I'm healed! I'm healed!" I lifted up her crutches above my head and shouted, at the top of my lungs to the people walking past, "Jesus has just healed this woman!" People stopped and stared, wondering what on earth was going on!

After a short talk with the young woman, she put the crutches on her shoulder and walked off down the street! I started to preach again, all the while keeping my eye on her as she walked away. After she had walked about fifty metres, she turned and smiled at me and put her thumb up, to show that she really was completely healed!

Reaching the Muslims

Mohammad was an angry Muslim who had taken offense to my preaching. His gang of about ten young Muslim men had started to heckle me as I was preaching, and so we got into a heated debate.

They kept shouting at me "Jesus isn't the Son of God, He is only a prophet!" The boldness of the Holy Ghost was upon me. "Jesus will show you that He is the Son of God- let me pray for you! Who has any pain in their body?" Mohammad put his hand up "I have a really painful hand!" He said "I wouldn't even be able to hold your Bible, it's so painful!" (My Bible was a pocket-sized Bible, very small.)

So, I gathered the gang of Muslims around and told them that Jesus was going to show them that He is the Son of God by healing Mohammad's hand. So, as they watched, I said a quick prayer and then thrust my Bible into Mohammad's out-stretched hand. He looked at his hand as he moved it around. "There's no pain!" He said in a shocked tone of voice. "But it will probably hurt again soon" he said. "No, it won't! Jesus has healed it!" I boldly declared.

The gang of Muslims, even though they all saw it happen, still continued to argue that Jesus wasn't the Son of God. Mohammad just sat there on a bench, no longer arguing but just staring at his hand as he continued to move it around.

A few weeks later, as I was preaching, I saw Mohammad walking past on the other side of the street. "Hey! Mohammad, how's your hand?" I shouted. He sheepishly raised it into the air and smiled and nodded, as if to say "Yes, it's still healed!"

Jesus always gets the victory!

As I preached in a regular spot, I got to see people going about their daily routines. I would see a lot of the same faces each day. There were two lads, who would walk past me each day. They would stand for a few minutes, listening and then off they went. They started to listen for longer as the days went past. This went on for about six weeks. I got talking to them. They were electricians, doing their apprenticeships at college.

One of them confessed to being a Muslim. I knew that the Lord had arrested his heart- he was captivated by The Word of God! He told me of his fears of converting to Christianity because he knew the cost involved-rejection from his family, and possibly worse! I said to him "Maybe the Lord wants to use you to bring the light into your family?" I could see that he thought deeply upon this, but he wouldn't commit to the Lord.

I prayed for him…

About two weeks later, I saw him coming up to me. I could tell by the smile on his face the news that he was going to tell me "I've given my life to Jesus!" he said! I was over-joyed! His friend wasn't having any of it! He said that he didn't believe.

The next time that I saw them, they came walking up to me and the ex-Muslim said "I have led my friend to the Lord!" His friend was stood there, with a beaming smile! How good our God is!

Another man who would walk past and stop for a while was a Mormon. I talked to him and invited him to my house, to attend my Bible study that I held every Wednesday and Friday. I could see that he had been indoctrinated, and that, on hearing the Living Word, that that stronghold would be cast down. God's Word is Living and powerful.

After a few months, he renounced Mormonism and has now written an extensive study on why Mormons should turn from their cult, and to put their faith in Christ of the Bible!

The one of the most dramatic transformations that I witnessed on the streets was with a young girl of about fourteen years old.

I was preaching one day, when I noticed a girl nearby, stood by herself, crying. The Lord said to stop preaching and to go over to her, so I did. I began to speak to her, and she told me that she had come from Slough with her mother to do some shopping, but her mother had gotten upset with her and so had just left her there on the street, and had gone home to Slough without her, leaving her stranded, with no money for the fare back.

The Lord told me to take her to the Police Point, so that they could take care of her, because just giving her the fare for her journey back would mean that she would be travelling alone, which was not wise. So, I took her by the hand and started to walk to the Police Point.

She was very upset and downcast and so she wasn't talking much, so I started to tell this poor child about the love of God Almighty for her. I told her the Gospel and explained why Jesus died for her. I told her to ask Jesus to reveal Himself to her, so that she may know that He is real and alive! I felt The Holy Spirit's presence and His great love for this young girl as I spoke to her. We soon reached our destination, and so I left her in the safe hands of the police.

About two weeks later I was preaching in another part of Swindon's town centre, when suddenly a young girl came running up to me, waving her arms in the air! "John! John!" she shouted as she approached me with a face full of joy. (Now, the Lord had given me a great gift for remembering peoples' faces and names. I may have only spoken to someone briefly on the streets and then I may not have seen them for years, and I would be able to remember their names and faces.)

But as the girl started to speak to me, I just looked at her blankly. "Do I know you?" I asked, "Have we spoken before?" I said "Yes!" she replied and then she continued to retell of our encounter two weeks earlier. I was shocked! She said "What you told me to do, to ask Jesus to show me if He was real, well, I did and it worked!" she excitedly exclaimed.

I was lost for words! The change in her whole appearance was dramatic-she was radiant! I just stood there, shaking my head, amazed at what the

Lord had done. We parted with a hug, and I walked home in a state of awe at the goodness of my God!

I was very well known to the police. There was always one particular policeman who would be sent to warn me about my preaching. Many times, the Holy Spirit would rebuke him as he tried to persuade me to "Tone it down a little!" I had a love for this man. I felt for him because I knew that he was only doing his job, but I could see the frustration in him as he struggled to understand why I did what I did.

One day he came up to me with a big grin on his face.

"Well done, John!" he said "You have been behaving yourself! We haven't had a complaint about you for the past two weeks!" He said, believing that I had finally taken his advice…

"Officer, I have been on holiday for two weeks and today is my first day back!" I replied with an even bigger grin!

He laughed and walked off, shaking his head!

But the police knew where they could come to when they needed help. A friend of ours, who was also a Christian, was very well known to the police, because she had tried to take her life on a number of occasions in the past. She was going through a hard time. My favourite policeman came walking up to me one day. "John" he said "You know such and such, don't you?" "Yes, she is a friend of mine" I replied. "We've been having some trouble with her" he said (meaning that she had been threatening to kill herself) "Really? I'll have to pray for her" I said.

Now, in the past, when she had tried to harm herself, they had locked her up in a secure hospital.

That night there was a knock at our door. I opened it up, only to see the police stood there with my friend. "Do you think that she could stay with you?" The police asked, because they knew that taking her to the hospital didn't do her much good, and so they had brought her to our house because they knew that Jesus would take good care of her! "Yes! Officer" I said and received the sister into our house. She stayed with us for three months. When the day came for her to leave, she confessed that, all the time that she had spent with us, she never once had a suicidal thought, but had only experienced peace within!

Praise the Lord for His loving kindness!

I was really blessed to know that the police had thought of bringing her to us instead of taking her to the hospital. I knew from then on, that my time on the streets was a great witness to the police.

Heartbreaking News

Big Dave would frequently turn up while I was preaching. He would stand there and do his favourite thing-smoke a cigar! I noticed that he was becoming more agitated by the preaching and started to become confrontational. I had seen it many times with Big Dave. I would go for a meal with him and let him talk about his problems.

But when he got ill he would not sleep and would become totally detached from reality! I felt sorry for him, because I had prayed so many times for him and yet he remained in a state of unbelief. He would say that he believed in Jesus, but as I would question him, it would always turn out that it wasn't Jesus of the Bible whom he believed in. He never seemed to let go of his spiritualism, because his Father died a spiritualist and he loved his Father and he knew that, if he renounced spiritualism, then he would have to face the truth of the fate of his Father...

One day as I was preaching, a friend of Big Dave came up to me. "Did you hear about Dave, John?" she said. "Did I hear what?" I replied "They found Dave dead in his flat. He had been dead for three days before they found him!" I was shocked! I walked home with a heavy heart.

This man, who I had vowed not to even get to know, had become such a close friend of mine, and yet, he had died alone, and had laid there for three days without anybody missing him... I felt that I had let Big Dave down. He used to annoy me because he would faithfully phone me every day- because he was just being a friend to me, and yet, I wasn't even aware that he hadn't phoned me for three days because I was too wrapped up in what I was doing to even notice.

I'm so sorry Big Dave.

Looking back on my time on the streets, it was such a precious time that the Lord gave to me. Even though, at times, it seemed to be a furnace of affliction with many hardships and much heartache, I would gladly do it all over again! And a thousand times more!

I have had the privilege to see the Lord do the miraculous, many, many times. Everytime that we preached, no matter where it was, there was always an uproar from the public. Swindon was turned upside down by the preaching of the Gospel!

I have seen hearts and lives changed forever by the power of the Gospel, including my own! I have seen people saved, healed and delivered by the Living God. Even though many people had accused me of doing it wrong, the Lord faithfully confirmed His Word with signs and wonders. I prayed for many, many people and every one of them confessed to being healed.

Only three people ever had said that they had felt no change after prayer (I didn't believe them!) I have felt God's love for the lost. The Lord has worked a great work in my life by changing me through the things that I have experienced. It is such a blessed life to live and walk with the Lord.

The Book of Acts is still being lived in the Believer's lives!

CHAPTER 7 ~ ISRAEL AND PAKISTAN

"For we which live are always delivered unto death for Jesus' sake..." - 2 Corinthians 4:11

A Jewish lady, whom I knew from Germany, contacted me and told me that the Lord had put it into her heart to send me to Israel to preach His Gospel. She sent me £1000. I calculated that this would be enough for me and my wife, Rachel, to go together and spend a week in Jerusalem, to preach and distribute Gospel materials. We would be staying on the top of The Mount of Olives, and every day, we would descend down into Jerusalem to evangelize, just like our Master had done two thousand years before.

We arrived in Israel with great excitement! The flight had lasted about five hours. When the Captain of the flight had announced that it was time for prayer, all of the Ultra-Orthodox Jews made their way to the back of the plane to pray for a safe landing and for blessings upon their journey. Rachel and I decided to join them, much to their astonishment, that two Gentiles would be bold enough to come and stand amongst them and pray! Some of them, I could tell by their faces, were greatly offended, whilst others seemed very pleased!

After we had collected our luggage, we caught a small bus to the hotel, which was situated on the very top of the Mount of Olives. We stopped off half way, to pick up some books that we were going to use for our outreach. The books were the testimony of an Israeli Christian, written in Hebrew, of how he had come to know Jesus as the Christ.

We were not in the dark about Jerusalem! It is a city that is a religious powder keg just waiting for someone to ignite the fuse and "Bang!" Big trouble! We knew that it was a highly dangerous place to openly preach the Gospel. Many prophets, and our own dear Lord, had been put to death there because of doing what we were going to do- to publicly proclaim the Gospel! You see, in the eyes of a religious Jew, an Evangelical Christian is worse than a terrorist, because, as they reason it, "a terrorist will just kill our people, but an Evangelical Christian will take our souls and send us to hell" We would need the Lord's wisdom and protection if we were to avoid conflict...

The first day of our small campaign was very exhausting. We had walked all around Jerusalem and back again! We visited all of the popular tourist sights, like the Garden Tomb, Golgotha, the City of David, etc. It was blisteringly hot. I was surprised by my lack of enthusiasm for the tourist sights. The Garden Tomb had a lovely, tangible peace in the air, but that was it- I was carrying within me the Living Christ, and so all of these things seemed rather dead to me...

All week we gave out these books. We had some wonderful, God-ordained conversations with both Jews and Palestinians. One old lady, near to the Kotel (The Western Wall) after having a quick look inside, started to shout and swear and threw the book at us, but on the whole, they were received without much fuss.

Then came the last day. We were evangelizing with the books in the Old City of Jerusalem when the Lord had told us that He wanted us to preach! So, we made our way to the Damascus Gate, because that was one of the busiest gates into Jerusalem. Jews, Muslims and Catholics all entered in through this gate, and so it would be an ideal place to preach the Gospel. I asked the soldiers if it would be okay to preach, and they said "Oh, yes! But preach down there..." motioning with their arms to preach in the new part of Jerusalem which was about a mile away because they knew what could happen if the people became upset! "Well is there any reason why I cannot preach right here?" I asked, to which they gave no real objection and so we went to prayer!

We asked the Lord to give us a window of opportunity, so that we could preach the Gospel without any interruptions or any persecution.

We preached for about twenty minutes! (We were told that, if you could preach for five minutes without any interruptions or persecution, you would have done well...) We preached against Judaism, Islam and Catholicism without the slightest disturbance!

Afterwards, whilst I was walking on the Temple Mount, I got talking to a man from England who was very excited because he had heard that some "Messianic Christians" had been preaching outside of the Damascus Gate (which, by the way, is not too far from where they had stoned Stephen, in the Bible, for doing the exact same thing!) "Oh, yeah! That was us!" I said, trying not to sound proud in any way. I marvelled at how quickly news travelled in this small, but beautiful city!

It wasn't long before we were back home, and I was reflecting upon our journey. I knew many mature Christians who would love to travel to Israel but had never been. "Lord, why did You take me to Israel and not these people who desire to go and are far more mature in their faith than I am?" I asked. The Lord's reply was simple and direct "Because I knew that you would preach My Gospel!'"

It was a grief to my heart to see so many Christians in Jerusalem, visiting the sights, etc, and yet not many of them were there to preach the Gospel...

The Battle of the Passport

Texan contacted me again. This time he had been invited by a Pastor in Pakistan, to bring a team with him and to put on a Healing and Deliverance Crusade for the people. I had met this Pakistani Pastor in Germany. He was a wonderful brother in the Lord, and we soon became very close friends. I will call him, "Pastor Hallelujah!" because, as he once explained to me, it was his favourite word when he had first come to know the Lord.

I was very excited at the thought of travelling to Pakistan to preach and to minister the Gospel, even though we had been warned by Pastor Hallelujah that it was a very dangerous country to share the Gospel in. He had told us of the many attempts upon his own life by the Muslims for preaching Jesus Christ, and also, it was widely known in the Christian Community and also on the world- wide news, that Christians were regularly being killed for their faith in Pakistan.

So, our eyes were opened for what we should expect, but it still came as a huge shock to me when reality struck!

The battle began as soon as I agreed to travel with Texan to Pakistan.

My dear father had been diagnosed with cancer earlier in the year and the devil said "If you go to Pakistan, you will never see your father alive again!" and so, I committed my father into the hands of my Heavenly Father, and believed that all would be well on my return...

I checked my passport, and I could see that it had plenty of time left on it to make the journey. I checked the Pakistani Embassy's website to make sure that I would send all the relevant information that was required with my application for a three-month visa. I went to the Post Office and was asked if I wanted to send it by Recorded Delivery, and being an expostman, I should have said "Yes" but I said "No!" and sent it by regular post...

About two weeks later, I was beginning to get a little anxious about the fact that I hadn't heard anything back from the Embassy because the time of my flights departure was drawing near. I had already paid £1100 to secure my place on the flight for the dates set by Texan and Pastor Hallelujah, and so I decided to phone the Embassy to check on how my application was coming along. "I'm sorry, sir, but we have no record of receiving any application from you..." came the horrifying reply! I couldn't believe it!

My application, along with my passport, had been lost in the post!! If only I had sent it by Recorded Delivery! I thought... Now I would have to apply for a new passport, as well as re-applying for the visa. There was simply not enough time to do it before my flight date. But I kept praying because I knew that The Lord had told me to go, and so it was settled in my heart that I would not give up until that plane took off...

The first thing to do was to get a new passport. The problem was that it usually takes about 4-6 weeks! I checked their website and found that you could obtain a "Fast track" passport if you went directly to the Passport Office. The nearest one to me was in London, and so I set out, the next day, on the outrageously expensive train into London.

Finances were very low because of the cost of the flight, but I had about £120 left in my account. When I arrived at the Passport Office, I filled out the relevant forms, but noticed that it said that if you had lost your passport, it would take a minimum of four days to obtain a new one! My heart sank... that would not leave enough time to be able to apply for my visa in time. I felt very disappointed, but there was a still small voice inside that kept prompting me to keep on believing that I would make it.

I approached the desk, armed with my forms and a heavy heart. I handed the forms to the woman, who glanced at them and then just looked me in the eyes and said "Would you like to have your passport today?" I was stunned! "I have lost mine and it says that it's a four day wait to get a new one" I replied. It was if she never heard anything that I had just spoken, but simply repeated "Would you like to have your passport today?" "Err...well... Yes! Please!" I replied with a hint of awe and wonder in my voice- I knew that God was with me and that He was moving all obstacles from out of my path!

The cost for the new passport was £120 which was all the money that I had, but I had a new passport and I still had a chance to make it...but there was another problem...

In order for me to get a visa from the Pakistani Embassy, it would require a five- day process, in which I would have to travel to the Embassy, in London, on the Monday, submit all the relevant information, and then it would be a five day wait, which would mean, again, that there wouldn't be enough time because my flight would be leaving on the Friday morning.

But I knew that God had made a way for me to get my passport, and so I was convinced that He would do the rest. The Lord told me to phone the Embassy and to get them to verbally confirm that I could have my visa on the Thursday, which I did and one of the staff confirmed that, if all the documents were prepared, then, yes, I could have it on the Thursday, even though that would be four days instead of the stipulated five!

I arrived at the Embassy on the Monday morning, full of excitement and joy, knowing that, all going well, on the Friday morning I would be leaving for an adventure in Pakistan! There was a huge queue waiting for visas, and so I joined the back and waited...and waited...and waited some more... Eventually I got to the front and was invited to sit down at a table with two stern looking officials, who were sat behind it. They quickly looked at my documents, and then just handed them back to me and said "No, sorry!" "What do you mean, No sorry!?" I asked. "You need to have your invitation letter from the Pastor to be signed by him" they said with an air of indifference!

Pastor Hallelujah had sent me an invitation letter but had not put his signature to it, which was a problem because now I would have to travel back home, scan and email the document to Pastor Hallelujah in Pakistan, wait for him to send it back and then travel back to London to begin the five-day application process again! Now it was impossible to make the Friday deadline, and yet, that still small voice inside of me would not let me rest. "Keep praying! keep praying!" would be the words resounding around inside of my heart.

The next day I joined the back of the queue that snaked across the Embassy's rear garden and waited...and waited...and waited some more....

Eventually I got to the front and proceeded to do as the day before. I sat down and handed them the documents, with the freshly printed off Invitation letter signed by Pastor Hallelujah (whilst he was out in the fields of Pakistan, preaching the Gospel!).

"No sorry!" they said as they threw the documents onto the table in front of me "What do you mean, No sorry!?" I said in disbelief. "We need to have the plans of your house, to verify your address" they said. "Are you kidding me? Why on earth would you need the plans to my house to verify my address? Surely some fuel bills with my name and address on it would suffice?" I reasoned. "We need the plans to verify that the house actually exists!" they replied.

"You couldn't make this stuff up!" I thought to myself and then I realised that these were devils speaking out of their mouths, and they were determined to stop me from going to Pakistan because they knew why I was going-it was stated on my application form, 'Reason for visit'..."To preach the Gospel!"

On the train back home, I was thinking about what had happened "They need the plans of my house, how ridiculous!" of course it was...satan was up to his tricks, to try and get me in a place of defeat, but I was still thinking about the miracles that God had already done to get me this far, and until that plane took off, it wasn't over...

Wednesday morning, the flight was leaving on Friday, and now I was heading back to the Embassy to begin the five-day application process for my visa all over again, once all the documents were verified to be acceptable.

I joined the back of the queue, and waited...and waited...and waited some more... I sat down at the table and handed them my documents, and held my breath..."OK, fine!" they said, without barely looking at them, and directed me into the Embassy building. I found the place where I was to hand in my verified documents and application. "Come back tomorrow! " was all that was said. I left wondering what was going to happen, but I couldn't help feeling that God was still going to do the impossible...

Thursday morning and I arrived at the Embassy. My plane was leaving the next day, Friday, and I was facing a five-day wait for my visa. I went to the relevant counter. "Yes, Mr Dunn, all of your documents are received and checked..." said the man behind the desk. "So when can I have my visa?" I asked. "Let's see, you handed in the documents yesterday, and so it would be Wednesday, next week..." He said.

Instead of disappointment in me, there came a righteous anger! I'd had enough of being pushed around by the demons that were operating through these men! "Look, mate," I said" I phoned last week and I asked if I could have my visa on the Thursday, and the man on the other end of the phone said "yes!" " Yes but" he said to try to interrupt me but I kept on going "You have messed me around all week! I've had to come up here every day because you found some petty reason why my documents were not acceptable- now I want my visa, and I want it today!" was roughly how the conversation went, to which the man behind the desk disappeared through a door to his right and I went and sat down and began to pray...

The man reappeared about ten minutes later. I walked up to the desk. He handed me a ticket and said very sheepishly "Come back at twelve." It was a receipt for my visa! Praise God! I was amazed at what the Lord had done. He had removed all of the obstacles that the enemy had put in the way to try and stop me. "He truly is in control of all things!" I thought to myself as I returned at twelve to collect my visa.

There was a different man waiting for me behind the desk, and he didn't look very happy when I handed him my receipt. He started to question me in a rough and blunt voice "Who said that you could have your visa today? It takes five days!" and on he went...

I kept calm and just prayed underneath my breath. I kept my eyes on the Lord. The storm soon passed, and this angry man was soon handing me a lovely, stamped, three- month visa for Pakistan! It had been a tough month, but the Lord had delivered my visa to me the day before my flight- such perfect timing, and against all odds! But I had my visa, and Pakistan was now in my sights...

Reality Bites

The arrangements were all made. It would be a five- day crusade in Pakistan, preaching and ministering the Gospel in the Christian areas as well as in the Muslim areas! Obviously, Texan was the one who was going to be doing the preaching- I was on the ministering team- helping to set up all of the gear and, obviously, praying for the people in the crusades. After Pakistan we were flying on to Malaysia for some more meetings.

My flight landed in Abu Dhabi airport, in the United Arab Emirates for the connecting flight into Lahore, Pakistan.

The airport was amazing- so clean and decorated with an amazing blue and white glass ceiling. It was the first time that I had been in a non-western culture. The men were walking around in their crisp white gowns, with their heads wrapped in red and white shemaghs.

I found the departure gate, hoping to see Texan and Aztec waiting for me, but their plane hadn't landed yet and so I was the only European in the midst of a sea of Pakistanis! It was a very strange feeling, but I had an insight to how it must have been for Pakistanis who came to my country back in the fifties. It is a daunting feeling to a minority surrounded by the majority of a different culture.

Soon I recognized two familiar faces in the crowd- Texan and Aztec. Aztec, due to his brown skin and black moustache, fitted in well with the crowd. "Not a bad thing," I thought, "if something happens in Pakistan and we have to make a run for it..."

I was stopped at the check-in desk. "What now?" I thought to myself. "You have been upgraded to Business Class" the woman said with a smile! When Texan boarded the plane and saw me sat down in Business Class, he walked past, shaking his head, saying "That's not right...that's not right!" "Sorry" I said with a huge grin on my face "Business Class people are not allowed to speak to Economy Class!"

It was a lovely flight into Lahore. I was laid on an electronic massaging bed the whole way, with as much fresh orange juice and snacks as I could eat!

It was about three o'clock in the morning when we landed in a dark and humid Pakistan.

Pastor Hallelujah met us at the airport and we were immediately whisked away into a car and driven along the dusty roads to a house of a brother where we would be staying for a few days.

The whole thing reminded me of my Ninjitsu days, where we would enter a place under the cover of darkness, moving with stealth from place to place, and then we would make an exit without anyone knowing that we had ever been...but there was no chance of that on this trip! Pastor Hallelujah had put up three thousand posters with our faces on, around the local areas, declaring the times and the places of all of our meetings.

106

This gave the Taliban, who were against our meetings and had threatened to kill us if we came to Pakistan, all the information that they needed...

We were woken up in the morning by an invitation for breakfast by our host. He was a wealthy man and so he had prepared a delicacy for breakfast...goat leg soup!

Texan, in his wisdom, passed on breakfast, but I was eager to enjoy new experiences in this wonderful culture. Aztec and I sat at the table and were engaged in small talk when my bowl was put in front of me. My eyebrows raised as I was confronted with goats' legs hanging out of my bowl, with the hooves still attached! Then a platter was placed in front of me- the goats head...just sat there... just staring at me as I began to reluctantly gnaw upon one of its legs. Aztec went through his breakfast with great gusto! must have something to do with his blood line, I thought...

Pastor Hallelujah had told us that the President of Pakistan had tried to cancel our meetings because it was such a dangerous time but had allowed them to continue when he was told that we were already on our way to Pakistan. The Taliban had recently attacked a police station and an Army barracks, causing havoc amongst the population. They were not afraid to attack anyone, anywhere at anytime... and we were on their hit list! So, the President had ordered that we were to be protected by the local police at our meetings.

We made sure that we were fully prayed up when it came to the first meeting- no one knew what to expect. There was a tension in the air as we drove along the manic roads to the first meeting. It was dark. Pakistan has a policy of turning off the electricity for so many hours a day because of the lack of power.

The meeting was out in the countryside in a Christian Community. There were no lampposts or street lighting as we pulled up at the venue. But what there was, was sixty-five armed bodyguards, courtesy of the Pakistani Government, waiting for us! They surrounded the venue, which was, basically, an area of ground with a wall around it.

I spotted one man walking around with a pistol in his hand, with the hammer cocked and his finger on the trigger! I thought to myself "If his nerves get the better of him and he squeezes that trigger a bit too tight, all hell will break out!" Because it was so dark, and there were so many people walking around with guns, that no one would be able to tell who was a terrorist and who was a bodyguard.

I felt as if I had just entered the Wild West!

We had to walk through a narrow opening in the wall to get into the venue. I wasn't ready for what I was about to experience. As we entered, suddenly we were caught in spot-lights, and there were hundreds of people cheering and applauding. As we made our way through the crowd to the platform, about four young girls, armed with baskets of rose petals, started to throw them over us and onto the ground in our path.

I felt very uncomfortable at such a welcome. It made me feel both, so welcomed, but at the same time, I felt very unworthy at such a glorious ceremony. They hung a garland of fresh rose petals around our necks, which, at the first opportunity that I could, I gave to one of the small children that was sat at the front of the crowd.

It seemed to take forever for the crusade to actually begin. There were so many people who were being introduced to the crowd that I began to wonder what the purpose of the meeting actually was?

One person who was sat on the platform with us was the local Imam- the head Muslim who was there to make sure that nothing was said to insult his religion. One word from this man, and many Christians could have lost their lives.

There was great pressure upon Texan to preach the Gospel of Jesus Christ without offending the Imam- and I saw that God gave him the grace and wisdom to do it!

It was a wonderful meeting- the power of God fell on the people and many testified to being healed- including the Imam! He had arrived at the meeting and was suddenly struck with a migraine headache. I saw Texan lay his hands on him and pray, and at the end of the meeting, the Imam confessed before all of the crowd that when he was prayed for in the Name of Jesus, he was instantly healed, much to his amazement!

The Christians were rejoicing and celebrating! They thanked us for coming to Pakistan at such a dangerous time, to be with them and to encourage them. They thanked us for not forgetting about them.

As we sat with the organizers after the meeting, they began to tell us that, during the meeting, two Taliban fighters had been arrested by security whilst trying to get into the venue with bombs in order to kill us and to kill as many Christians as they could (because the venue was just a wall surrounding a patch of ground, it would have been very easy for them to have thrown the bombs over the wall and into the midst of the people!)

They suggested that we should cancel the meeting that was due to be held the next day, saying that it was too dangerous. But Texan gave them a brief summary of all of the persecution that he had faced over the years, and so, when they heard that they simply said "Oh! Okay then, we'll continue!"

That night I could barely sleep. My mind was going over all of the reports that I had seen on the news about the Taliban, and now this was reality...They were after ME... like... little me, the nobody from Great Bedwyn, was actually a target for terrorists!

It was a huge shock, that this was real and not a game and that, I could actually be killed at any moment for the sake of Christ! That, if there was any trouble, that there was nowhere to run or hide. I stood out like a sore thumb. But, then I remembered all of the miracles that the Lord had done just to get me to Pakistan! and so, I figured, that there was a chance that I would survive and make it home again to Great Bedwyn. The Pakistani Christians didn't have that hope- they lived under the threat of death twenty-four seven!

In order to truly follow Christ, it really does mean that you have to lay down your life for His glory.

I prayed until about four o'clock in the morning. We were staying in the only hotel in the area (actually, it was the only building in the area!) The windows and doors were all barred, so there was only one way out of the building- the front door. We had one, armed bodyguard sleeping outside of our door. It wouldn't have been that hard to have found us...I talked to Texan, and told him that I had difficulty in sleeping, who then prayed for me, and the Lord graciously strengthened me and placed His peace in my heart.

The next meeting was to be held in the daytime. The Taliban knew where we were. They had tried to kill us the previous night. "What will the day bring forth?" I thought to myself as we made our way to the meeting. We had to drive down some extremely narrow streets in order to reach the venue. Texan, being an ex- Special Forces soldier, said that we were sitting ducks.

Only the Lord could keep us alive...

Continuing On

We smiled at each other as we pulled up at the venue, with a mutual acknowledgement of the danger that we were in and that this might be the time of our Home-calling! It was time to enter into the den of lions once again...

About two hundred people had gathered for the meeting. They were all sat down in the dust, eagerly waiting for the Lord to move again- and they were not disappointed! I had felt so vulnerable at the hotel, but now, in the meeting with the presence of God, I felt safe. It had nothing to do with the fact that we had a lot of armed bodyguards patrolling around the perimeter of the venue, although that was a small comfort!

As I sat in the front of the meeting, setting up the sound equipment, I noticed a man walking in to the meeting carrying a boy of about twelve years old. The boy's limbs were completely limp and I remember thinking that he looked like a big rag doll by the way that his arms and legs just swayed around as he was carried by his Father.

The man made his way to the front and laid the lad in the dirt, right in front of where Texan would be preaching.

About half way through the preaching I noticed, out of the corner of my eye, that there seemed to be a commotion near the front. I stood up to see what was going on because there seemed to be a cloud of dust being whipped up by someone. The Holy Spirit had fallen, and His power had hit that paralysed boy, who was now thrashing around on the ground and bouncing up and down.

Suddenly the boy jumped to his feet and just stood there with a look of shock and confusion on his face! He had no idea what had just happened to him, only that, one minute he was led on the ground, paralysed, and the next, he was standing up and everyone was looking at him!

After the meeting there was an open mic for people to come and share their testimonies of what the Lord had done for them. There were quite a few people who shared various healing testimonies from the previous nights meeting, then the Father of that lad came forward and shared how his son had been completely paralysed for six years and had now been totally healed! I saw this with my own eyes! (I also have the whole thing caught on video.)

We were invited by one of the organizers to have dinner with him and his family. We drove to his house and entered a courtyard where there were women busy preparing tables and chairs. As we sat talking, I noticed a woman over the other side of the courtyard, stood over a little fire, huddled under a small tin roof, making bread. She looked very lonely, and the bread smelled so nice that I decided to go over to her and talk to her, so that she would feel appreciated for her hard work.

As I talked to her, I noticed that the hands and wrists of this old lady were black and textured like leather where they had been burned so many times as she had thrusted them into the fire to turn the bread over. She asked me to pray for the skin on her arms to be healed.

Suddenly I noticed that all of the men were dragging their seats over to where we were and sitting down and talking together. I had no idea of the culture, but apparently, the men and women remain separate when preparing for and entertaining guests. The women do all the cooking and remain out of sight.

The Organizer, when he had seen me go over to the woman, had panicked because it was another man's wife and he didn't know what to do! This Westerner was going against the customs of their culture. I thought that it was funny, to see everyone crowded underneath a small tin roof, huddled around a small fire, when there was a large, open courtyard in which to sit in!

The next meetings that we were to minister in were to be held in Islamabad. This would be in a totally Muslim area. (This would mean that we would be taking the "battle to the gate!" Isaiah 28:6) On the way there we would be driving past the Christian village where the Muslims had locked the Christians in their houses and then burned them down to the ground killing many of our brothers and sisters and their children. This had happened only a few months before we arrived.

This was going to be interesting...

We pulled up to our hotel and were met by the local police, who had been assigned to be our bodyguards- they were all Muslim! Not only were they Muslim, but they were Muslims with big guns! Think about that- Muslims assigned to protect Christians from attacks by Muslims because they were preaching what all Muslims consider to be blasphemy! I didn't have much faith in my bodyguards- they didn't seem to be very friendly. Actually, some of them looked very resentful to be assigned to look after us! It was a bit un-nerving to think that, at any moment, one of them could have turned his gun upon us! (Which they had been known to do in the past- to shoot the person that they were assigned to protect.)

I kept my eyes on Jesus...

That night we had the meeting in the Muslim's backyard! The venue was, again, just a large area of open ground that had blocks of flats on either side of it. They had erected a stage at one end of the land. It would had been very easy for anyone to have shot at us from the flats.

It felt like Duck Hunting season was about to begin again!

During the meeting the Lord Jesus showed up with great power to heal and to deliver. Many people manifested demons coming out of them.

At one point, there were so many people being prayed for on the platform, that it felt like it was going to collapse! This area, although totally Muslim, was very open to the Gospel on the account of a mighty miracle that had happened...

Pastor Hallelujah had held a crusade there a few months before and a Muslim family had heard about the miracles that were taking place, and so they brought their sick baby to the meeting. During the meeting, the baby had actually died, and so they were leaving when someone had told Pastor Hallelujah about their situation. He called them up to the platform and boldly proclaimed before the crowd that Jesus could raise the dead!

Now this was in front of many Muslims, that, if nothing had happened, he probably would not have made it out of there alive... but the Lord is faithful to His servants, and so, when the Pastor lifted up the baby and prayed, the child was raised from the dead! In their joy, the Muslims had invited Pastor Hallelujah back to do some more crusades, and that was why we were having that meeting in that particular place...

Walking Boots

We also attended another meeting, but this was on a smaller scale. It was to be held in a local church. As we approached the building, I noticed a pile of shoes by the entrance doorway. Pastor Hallelujah explained that we would have to leave our shoes outside. I was wearing a lovely pair of black, Texan Cowboy boots, with decorative silver trims on the toes and heels, that Texan had bought for me as a gift when I went to Texas.

Texan flatly refused to leave his Cowboy boots outside, saying that if the boots didn't enter the building, then neither did he!

I thought this was a bit harsh, and so I took mine off and left them outside. "Don't worry, Mr John, we will look after them for you.." they said...Texan entered the Church, clutching his boots. The meeting was blessed and the Lord poured out His power.

I was the only one praying at the end, nearly everybody else had gone. The lad that I was praying for had a painful leg. The Lord graciously healed him. "Time to go!" Texan exclaimed, and marched to the door. There were no shoes outside of the church door... neither were there any black, Texan Cowboy boots with the silver trims! They had obviously gone for a walk without me!

Pastor Hallelujah was greatly disturbed by this. It was a great embarrassment to that church. I had to walk back to the car, through the dusty streets, in my socks!

We drove to the shops because they wanted to buy me a new pair of shoes, but I told them that it was not necessary. Texan decided that he wanted to have a haircut and so we went into a Muslim barbershop. Texan had quite a sense of humour, and so, whilst I was having a shave by the Muslim barber, as he held the cut-throat razor to my throat, Texan loudly asked me "Do you think that now would be a good time to tell him that you're a Christian?" I gulped and smiled awkwardly in the mirror! At the exact same time, a fly flew up my nose, and it was only by the grace of God that I didn't shake my head or move one inch!

That night Aztec and I had to share a bed in the hotel. At the bottom of the bed sat a huge Muslim police officer, with a great big orange beard, armed with an even bigger AK47 machine gun! I talked to him a lot, but all he could say was "I... like you! ...I ...like you!" to which I would respond "I like you too, because you have an AK47 and I don't!" to the which he would laugh and nod his head, not understanding anything that I had said! He sat there all night, bless him, ready to protect us from any harm. As I drifted off to sleep I thought of God's faithfulness to protect us. "Who would have thought that, sometimes, the Lord's angels come to your aid, armed with an AK47!"

Because of the miracles of healings that were being done, and the fact that many Muslims were coming to the meetings, news of these meetings caught the attention of the President of Pakistan, who personally invited us to have lunch with representatives of his Government. And the question that these, all-Muslim Government representatives asked us four Christians was "How can we, as a Government, make Pakistan a better country?" The Lord had opened a mighty door for us to share Christ with them. The meeting with the Government made the local, national and international news (Courtesy of CNN News!) The Media tried to portray our meetings that we were holding in Pakistan as "Interfaith" meetings, but they weren't- we were there to win Muslims to Christ!

It soon became time for us to leave Pakistan and head for Malaysia. As I stood in line waiting to board the plane, I was in awe of what the Lord had done- He had made the way for me to get my passport against all odds.

He had made a way for me to get my visa, against all odds. When all the other Christian meetings were shut down in Pakistan, because of the danger, He had made a way for ours to continue. He made a way for us to hold meetings in totally Muslim areas and hundreds had attended!

He had protected us from an attempt by the Taliban to kill us with bombs. He had advertised our meetings openly to the Talban, who were unable to do anything about it! He had opened the door for us to share Christ with the all- Muslim Government of Pakistan, after being personally invited by the Muslim President himself and had put it in all of the newspapers and on the international news!

He had provided bodyguards for us that were Muslim, in a Muslim nation, so that we could preach Christ! He had healed and delivered many people, both Christian and Muslim. He had glorified His great and holy Name in Pakistan!

Texan turned to me and smiled- "We made it out alive!" He said, as we boarded the plane. I sighed a huge sigh of relief, praying that I would never have to go back to Pakistan again.

Apparently, the Lord never heard that prayer…

When I got home I had a phone call from my father, which was a miracle in itself, because my father never phoned anyone! (Before I had left for Pakistan, my father had phoned me to tell me that, if I was to keep sharing my faith with him when I came to see him, that I would not be welcome to come to his house anymore. I knew that this wasn't from my father's heart, but only a ploy by the enemy to stop my father from being saved, and so, it didn't hurt me and there was no bitterness in my heart towards my father. Instead I gave it to the Lord in prayer.)

My father said to me on the phone "John, could you come and see me- I need to talk to you about something..." The devil immediately said "He's going to tell you that he has only a few weeks to live. He's going to die in his sins and perish!" I rebuked his lies.

I arrived at my father's house and went into the bedroom, where he was sat up in bed. I closed the door. My father started to speak...

"John, whilst you were in Pakistan, I had been thinking about all you have told me about Jesus. There was a day in which I was in great pain- the painkillers that I have been taking weren't having any effect, and so I was in agony. Then in the midst of the pain, I simply cried out to Jesus 'Lord, if You are real, please help me!' and instantly, all the pain left my body! And now I know that it is the truth that you have been telling me! Son, would you like to pray for me?" And so, with tears flowing down my face, I led my dear father to his Saviour!

(Oh! Lord! You are so wonderful!)

I could see the genuine conversion in my father's heart. I would visit him in hospital and ask him what he had been doing that day. Many times he would reply to me "I've been confessing my sins to my Lord! I realise that you don't get away with anything!" It was music to my ears! My father had carried a lot of hurt and unforgiveness towards his mother. We talked about this, and I led him through a prayer for his mother. It was wonderful to hear my father praying to forgive her for all that she had done to him. He said to me "Do you know, John, this cancer has been a blessing to me, because through it I have found the Truth!"

That is a statement that can only come from a true convert!

When it came time for my father to go to his Heavenly Father, I was alone with him in the hospital. He looked at me and tried to speak but he was too weak and too medicated that he couldn't form the words. I was intent on praying for him, and so, I wasn't really speaking to him, but praying for him. I suddenly noticed that his breathing was growing very faint, and so I held his hand as he departed to his heavenly home.

Over the next few weeks, I couldn't help thinking to myself "I should have just spent the final hours being with my Father and talking to him, rather than praying for him." I asked the Lord "Father, could you tell my

Dad that I'm sorry for not just being there for him in the hospital...." I knew that the Lord would tell my Dad.

About two weeks later, I was in Germany praying with a German brother for a man who had some issues. We were both quite exhausted afterwards, and so we were both sat on a bed. My German brother was talking to me about something- I wasn't really paying close attention, when he suddenly turned to me and looked me straight in the eye and said "Your father forgives you!" and then he just carried on talking as if nothing had happened.. I was overjoyed! I knew that the Lord heard my prayer, and, because He is so lovely and faithful, He had spoken by His Spirit through His servant to bring me comfort and assurance of where my father was.

I know that my father is in Heaven with my Lord!

Back to the Holy Land

The Lord opened the door for me to return to Israel. My daughter, Keeleigh, had been invited by the Israeli Christian, whose books Rachel and I had given out in Jerusalem, to go to Israel and spend three months working with his team, to evangelize and to work in his hotel. It was a great opportunity for her to travel and see the world- especially, to see the Holy Land! I will call him Boldheart, because this dear brother was a great preacher, who fearlessly preached the Gospel in the streets of Israel, and so I had great respect for him, as one street preacher to another, for Israel can be a dangerous place to preach the Gospel in.

My flight landed in Ben Gurion Airport, Tel Aviv. I waited in line and eventually reached Passport Control. The conversation went as follows...

P.C "Passport please"

Me ...hands over passport...

P.C "Reason for your visit"

Me "Tourism"

P.C "Do you know anyone in Israel?"

Me "Yes, I know a Jewish man who owns a hotel in Tel Aviv."

P.C "And how did you meet him?"

Me "In church."

P.C "I'm sorry, did you say that you met him in church?"

Me "Yes"

P.C "I thought that he was a Jewish man that you knew in Tel Aviv?"

Me "He is Jewish!"

P.C "What on earth was he doing in a church!!"

Me "He believes in your Messiah, Jesus!"

P.C (looking confused and indifferent) reaches for and presses a buzzer...

Security "Would you like to step this way, Mr. Dunn. We have some questions for you..."

And so, I was ushered into a side room, to wait for about half an hour before being interviewed... The man to whom I spoke had an American accent. He was very polite and respectful with his questioning and with his tone of voice.

"I see you have been to Pakistan" He said "What was the reason for your visit?" he asked. "I went to tell them about your God! The God of Abraham, The God of Isaac and The God of Jacob" I replied with a confident voice, knowing that the Lord had given me an opportunity to share Christ with this man. His eyebrows raised "Really?" he said with a smile and so I continued to tell him all about Pakistan and the Lord Jesus Christ.

At the end of the interview, he shook my hand as he gave me back my passport and said "Welcome to Israel! I hope you enjoy your stay!"

It was lovely to see my daughter again, whom I hadn't seen for nearly three months. We were to stay in a house that was owned by Boldheart, in the old port town of Jaffa. It was used as a place where the believers could live together in fellowship, who had come to Israel to evangelize and preach the Gospel. It had many bedrooms and so it could accommodate up to fifty people!

I met many lovely brothers and sisters from all over the world as I stayed there-Gary from Scotland, Almira (Babushka!) from Russia, Danuta from New Zealand, Ziv and Katya from Israel, Amy from Australia, Anthony from America, Priscilla from Portugal to name but a few! It was hosted by a lovely family who had moved from South Africa to evangelize the people of Israel. The husband's name was Israel, who was Jewish and originally came from the Galilee, and his wife's name was Marti, who was South African. Along with their children Yonathan, David and Gabriella, they stayed in the house and organised the outreaches.

Not long after settling in, Keeleigh told me about her room mate and the problems that she was having. It seemed as though the enemy was at work, because, apparently, when everyone was out of the house and this Polish woman was there by herself, things would move around the room by themselves. I could discern demonic activity by being in her presence and observing her body language and by the way that she was speaking. She seemed to be very tense and anxious. I had seen it before... She was desperate to be free and so, with a heart glowing with love and compassion for her, I agreed to pray for her. I was always excited to see what Jesus would do and how He would glorify His Name!

There was a woman from South Africa who also wanted to pray for her, to which she agreed. Israel and Marti had also asked me if I could pray for her. "Come and see the Lord get the victory!" I said to them but the Polish woman only wanted myself and the South African woman to be in the room. She was a bit overwhelmed by it all, but very desperate to be free.

I sat her down and asked her about her past. The open door by which the enemy had been able to gain entrance soon became obvious. Her mother was one of the top clairvoyants in Poland and had dedicated her daughter to do the same work, and to continue after she was gone.

This woman had told me that she was so accurate in telling the future, that she herself, was already in great demand in Poland. "Jesus is going to tear it all down! "I thought to myself.

I started to lead her in a prayer of renouncement, repentance and forgiveness when, all of a sudden, the South African woman interrupted and said "You don't need to do all of that... here, let me pray" she said and started to lay hands on the woman. The Lord spoke to me "Just let her do her thing, John. Be patient" and so I sat back and watched.

After praying this and that, she said "Now you are free!" But the Polish woman looked at me and said with great sadness and despair "But nothing has changed!"

This woman was twenty-nine years old, and for all of her life she had heard voices in her head, and they had not stopped after this woman had prayed for her.

So, I said, "Okay, now let me pray for you". I knew that the Lord would set her free. I could feel the excitement of the Holy Ghost inside of me. He loves to glorify Jesus! I led her through a simple prayer again and then I laid my hands on her and commanded that devil to come out of her in the Name of Jesus! She coughed and then, with a look of astonishment on her face, she exclaimed "They've stopped! They've stopped! The voices have stopped!" Jesus had totally set her free!

I stayed for two weeks and I watched her closely as we went out on outreaches, and as we went about everyday life. She was very relaxed and full of joy. She was completely set free!

Not too long after arriving back home in Poland she was baptized in the Holy Ghost. She shared her testimony on YouTube.

Israel and I decided to go to the local market place to do some outreach. We had some Gospel tracts in Hebrew and Arabic, so that we could reach as many people as we could. We were intending to evangelize one-on-one.

The market was an extremely busy place. People hurrying to and fro. Lots of noise and smells and beautifully coloured fruit, the which I had never seen before. We walked the length of the market, and as we came to a crossroads the Lord spoke to me "I want you to preach right there" He said, highlighting a place in the middle of the busy crossroads of people. I tried to ignore His voice. I wasn't too sure what Israel's reaction would be if I suddenly started shouting out the Gospel.

The place was busy, and we were by ourselves, so Israel and I continued on walking. We reached the end of the market, and so, we turned around and proceeded to walk back in the direction by which we had come. We reached the crossroads. "Are you going to preach or are you going to be disobedient?" The Lord asked. I took a deep breath "Ok, Lord, I'll preach."

I told my intentions to Israel, who, with a big smile on his face, said that he would stand near to one of the stalls and watch for the people's response. If there was anyone that would stop and listen, then he would go over and start a conversation with them.

So, I stood in the crossroads and lifted up my voice for the glory of my God. Whenever I preached, I gave it my all! The boldness of the Holy Ghost would always fall upon me as soon as I opened my mouth.

The people thought that I was crazy! Some laughed, some jeered, but some stopped and listened. I saw that Israel was busy talking to an Israeli woman who had stopped to listen. After I had finished, I joined him and spoke to the woman. She asked for prayer for an illness that she had. We prayed for her and went on our way looking for more people to share the Good News with. It was a miracle in itself, that a Jewish person, after hearing the Gospel would allow you to pray for them in the Name of Jesus- only the Lord could open someone's heart to allow this!

During my time in Israel, the Lord blessed me with many conversations with both Jews and Arabs.

Boldheart had a TV programme that went around the world, and I was blessed to be able to share the scriptures in two of those programmes.

Every Sabbath, Boldheart's ministry would go on outreach at the local beach in Tel Aviv. On a number of occasions I was able to preach to the people walking by.

On one such occasion, we had been sharing the Gospel opposite the beach. I had been handing out tracts but had not preached. As I made my way back to the house, walking with a South African brother, I noticed, at the end of the sea front, that there was a circle of chairs, and the people who were sat on them were taking it in turns to speak into a microphone.

As I looked, a woman with a clipboard under her arm, noticed me and came walking over to me. "What's going on?" I asked her. "This is an open discussion." She said." We are seeking reconciliation between Jews and Arabs. Theses people on the chairs have had their lives affected, in some way, by terrorism, and we are seeking suggestions on how to bring peace between Jews and Arabs. Do you have any suggestions?" she asked! "Do I!" I said and so I continued on to explain to her Jesus, the Prince of Peace.

I was expecting her to say "No, I'm sorry, that's not what were looking for…" But she didn't! She thought for a moment and then said "Would you like to share that with the group?" "Give me the mic!" I said, eager to glorify my God! and as they sat and listened, I preached Jesus, the Prince of Peace to them through an Interpreter. As soon as I finished, I handed back the microphone and walked off without saying another word or waiting for their response. My job was done.

My South African brother said "Wow! That was great!" "Yes! Praise God!" I replied with an air of satisfaction in my voice, knowing that the Lord had just done a great work by sharing His Word of reconciliation and His Word of Truth. What wonderful opportunities He gives us to share His love with others...

Oh! He is altogether lovely!

The Lord has allowed me to return to Israel on many occasions to preach His wonderful Gospel to both Jews and Arabs. It is such a privilege to be about His business.

Pakistan Revisited

Pastor Hallelujah had been busy in Pakistan. He had built a church in Lahore, in a Muslim neighbourhood, just down the street from their mosque. He had established a Bible School and had contacted me and asked if I would like to come and teach in his school. At the same time, we had established a Sewing School through a local Pastor in Sahiwal, in the south of Pakistan, and he was asking me to come and visit and to preach the Gospel in some meetings that he would arrange.

I had a growing sense of excitement to travel back to Pakistan, and I knew that it wasn't from me...The Holy Spirit was growing excited by what He was planning to do!

But, Pakistan! Really? To return, this time, meant that it would be just me. For two weeks, teaching in the Bible school and holding open air preaching meetings. Did I have the courage? No. Did I have a desire to return? No. Did I have an excuse not to go? No. The Lord was moving. He was stirring me up inside. I knew that the Holy Spirit would give me the courage. He was already creating in me the overwhelming desire to go...

I said "Yes!" to the Lord, I would go! The only window for me to go and teach in the Bible School would co-inside with a dangerous time in Pakistan when there was great trouble between the Sunni Muslims and the Shi-ite Muslims. It was so bad that the Government cut all communications for three days across the land. You couldn't phone anyone... The police, the Fire Brigade... no one. It was so that no one could plan any attacks against each other...The people tended to just stay indoors until it is over!

As if it wasn't dangerous enough already, the night before I was due to fly to Pakistan, I saw on the news that the Americans had decided to assassinate the leader of the Taliban!... Great, just what I didn't need to hear! The whole country was put on red alert, due to the expectation of retaliation by the Taliban.

"Will you still go?" The Lord asked. "It's about as dangerous as it can get" He said. "I will go on one condition, Lord... that you will show me Your power!" I replied. Something told me that I wasn't going to be disappointed but in a way that I hadn't expected...

When Pastor Hallelujah picked me up from the airport, he told me that the country was on high alert. Apparently, the Secret Service was pulling their hair out at the news that a foreigner was coming to preach the Gospel at this time! They were assigned to follow us. We were promised to have armed police to provide security at our meetings. Pastor Hallelujah also told me that the Taliban had issued a statement, declaring that they were going to attack the churches...Great!

The Pastor drove me to the church that he had built. It was a beautiful building. It had the highest steeple in the area, with a golden cross on the top, standing above all of the other surrounding buildings. It was going to be a busy two weeks. I was to teach each day in the Bible School. Then preach in some meetings in the evening. Then we were going to head for Jarranwala, a witchcraft stronghold, to have a few meetings, then back to Lahore, then on to Sahiwal in the south to preach in some open- air crusades, then back to Lahore to teach in the Bible school.

There was a packed room as I taught in the Bible School. It was a real privilege to be able to teach these precious brothers and sisters. They were all very keen to learn. They all had a heart for the Lord.

After teaching for a few hours, there was a meeting to be held by one of the students in their house. He had quite a large courtyard, which was completely filled with people as I made my way to the front to preach. Pastor Hallelujah was to be my Interpreter. I preached for about forty-five minutes and then prayed for anyone who wanted prayer- I was there for a long time because many people came forward. The night ended with a lovely meal provided by the host and his wife.

Jarranwala

After another few days of teaching, we were to head off to Jaranwala, to have some open-air meetings. I was excited and nervous at the same time! As we drove along the dusty, bumpy roads, Pastor Hallelujah informed me that the Taliban had declared that they had sent out twelve suicide bombers to blow up the churches in the Punjab area. "What area are we in?" I asked. "The Punjab" was the reply… Oh! just great!

We stopped off at a garage on the way. I needed to use the toilet, and as I got out of the car, I noticed two armed men sat down guarding the Petrol Station. The Lord spoke to me "Don't speak a word to them" He said. So, I walked straight to the toilets, not paying any attention to the voices of the men who were trying to speak to me. My two bodyguards also followed me. When we got back into the car, as we were driving down the road, they told me that the armed men had asked them "Is he a European? Is he a European?" My bodyguards had told them that I was from Afghanistan! (Apparently, there is a race of people from Afghanistan that have white skin and blue eyes, and so they look very European). If I had tried to speak to the armed men, they would have known that I was from Europe, and may well have shot me! No wonder the Lord had told me not to speak a word to them.

We got to Jarranwala and soon found the house at which we would be staying. It was quite late and the first meeting was due to be held the next day. But we soon found out that the police had cancelled it, because it was too dangerous to proceed with any meetings. I had to stay in the house, and not venture outside. I was the only white face in a sea of brown- it wouldn't have been too hard to have spotted me! So, a secret meeting was arranged for the night time.

It had been a long day and now it was time to get some sleep. We all slept in the same room. Pastor Hallelujah and I in a double bed, and the Two bodyguards on the floor, along with a few other men from the local church, who had joined us.

I woke in the middle of the night, needing to go to the toilet. So, I tip-toed over the bodyguards, who were both sound asleep on the floor. "Some kind of bodyguards…" I thought to myself as I crept into the bathroom.

Now earlier in the evening, I had seen the owner of the house spraying something into the bathroom. I had no idea what he was doing. But to my horror, I soon put two and two together!

Over the hole in the ground, where you had to squat down to go to the toilet, was a bees' hive behind some panelling. The man had obviously been spraying something to kill the bees because now, right where I had to squat were hundreds of bees, dead or dying, on the floor…Great!

As I was squatting there, the bees were still dropping down from above my head, down my back and onto the floor. Hundreds were crawling around my bare feet. I was praying for God's mercy! "I'll be laughing about this tomorrow!" I kept saying to myself, in order to keep myself calm, which isn't easy when you're facing the prospect of being stung by hundreds of bees in your private parts!

God had mercy upon me! I emerged from the bathroom sting free!

The next day was spent relaxing (If that was possible!) and waiting for the start of the secret meeting in the evening. One man turned up at the house, holding a little girl of three years old. They both seemed so joyful to see Pastor Hallelujah. Then the Pastor introduced me to them. "You see this little girl?" he asked "Well, she died for half an hour. They examined her and did all of the medical tests on her. She was dead. And so, the Father brought her to me. I prayed for her, and the Lord raised her from the dead!" He said it so matter-of-factly!

I was amazed at the love and respect that the people had for Pastor Hallelujah- it was something that I was not used to, coming from the West. Whenever the Pastor would sit down, young men would eagerly come to him and massage his feet or his shoulders. They would do this with a look of great privilege and pleasure on their faces! The unity and sense of family in Pakistan amongst the believers was genuine and humbling. These people had nothing, but when you would go to their homes to visit them, they gave you everything. And they did it joyfully! When I was among these people, I was reminded of the scripture;

"Hath not God chosen the poor of this world rich in faith…" (James 2:5a)

The Lord had put a great love and respect, deep within my heart, for the Christians of Pakistan.

It soon became dark outside. It was time to prepare to leave for the secret meeting. I was dressed in traditional Pakistani dress- a long, thin, cotton smock or shirt, with baggy trousers, sandals and, most importantly, my Bible! (Where ever we went in Pakistan I kept my Bible close to me! This brought me great comfort.)

We climbed into the car, and slowly made our way down the bumpy tracks. There were no streetlights. It was pitch black.

We drove for about half an hour and then the car suddenly came to a halt. We all got out of the car as quietly as we could. I couldn't see in front of my eyes, it was so dark. We made our way into a building. There were no lights on, everything was in total darkness. Somebody turned on their mobile phone, and for an instant there was light! "Turn that off!" came the quiet rebuke from somewhere in the room. We sat there for a few minutes. I could feel the tension in the air. We were waiting for the "All clear" before we moved out of the building.

When we finally did, it was completely black and silent outside. We began to walk across some fields, or open land. I was trying to concentrate on putting my feet onto solid ground and not to stumble into some pot-hole.

After about ten minutes I could hear some faint music in the distance, that started to grow louder with every step. Suddenly we stepped out of the darkness and into bright lights! I immediately noticed that, even though the police had cancelled our meeting in the day time, saying that it was too dangerous, that there were about six armed policemen there amongst the people. Pastor Hallelujah told me that they had been "hired" for our protection. I remember thinking that they all looked the same- green jumper, brown trousers, black hat with a matching black moustache! For some reason they all looked like Saddam Hussein...

The meeting place was just two parallel brick walls, about twenty-five feet apart. A platform had been erected at the far end, and it was filled with people worshipping the Lord. There was a sea of vibrant colour from the beautiful garments that the women wore. I was told that they had been worshipping for about two hours already!

I noticed two Christians with machine guns patrolling on top of the two walls. The atmosphere was electric! God's people were filled with such joy to be there. It was so humbling to see! These Christians that were there, were under the threat of being killed by the Taliban in this meeting, and yet, they were worshipping the Lord with huge smiles on their faces, dancing and praising His Name. I thought of the Sunday services that I had attended back in England, and the Lord opened my eyes to the vast difference between life and death. Here the church was living, because it was dying daily, whilst back in England, the church was dead because it was living...

I was alive! The Spirit of God was moving and to preach was so easy!

As I began, I noticed that at the very back of the meeting, a man walked in, clothed all in black, and it looked like, from his body language, that he was hiding something beneath his blanket that was wrapped around him. He had a very uncomfortable look on his face. I kept my eye on him as I preached.

The Lord was very gracious and poured out His power. Many were healed of various complaints and ailments and some gave their lives to the Lord. Then, as the end of the meeting approached, Pastor Hallelujah, who had been interpreting for me, said quietly to me "Now tell the people to close their eyes in prayer, and bow their heads. If someone is going to attack, it will be now, at the end of the meeting. We'll sneak out as they are praying!" It sounded like wise counsel to me, and so I asked the people to close their eyes and bow their heads, and as they did, Pastor Hallelujah and I tip-toed through them. As we did I kept my eye on the man in black at the back, waiting for any sign of movement from him but there wasn't any...

Sahiwal

We were soon back in the car and driving back to Lahore through the night so that we could leave for Sahiwal on the Monday. I was so filled with the Holy Ghost that I couldn't sleep but was replaying the days events over and over in my head. What a day it had been! What an adventure! And, praise God, He had more in store for me...

The drive down to Sahiwal was a long one. Three hours of driving on the crazy, haphazard roads of Pakistan! We were driving in Pastor Hallelujah's car. The back windows had been blackened out so that people could not look in and see a white man sat there!

As we drove along I noticed huge buses overtaking us filled with men with turbans and long black beards. "Do you know who they are, John?" Hallelujah asked. "No idea!" I said. "They are Taliban fighters. They are returning from a large meeting that they have just been holding. There was one hundred thousand of them, in that meeting..." he said.

I Was shocked! I thought that the Taliban was just a few radicals running around causing trouble, but they were not-they were huge in numbers! I watched bus after bus go pass us, loaded with these men. "Don't look at them, John. Keep your back to them" came the wise advice from Hallelujah. It was a bit intimidating to think of the vast number of Taliban that were passing me, just outside of my car door. Anyone of them would have been delighted to shoot me, just for being a white European! A prize trophy for them...

After about two hours of driving, Pastor Hallelujah asked "Are you hungry? Do you want to stop for some food?" "Yes!" I replied "That would be good" "Okay, we'll stop here" he said, pointing to a restaurant that was by the side of the motorway. It had tables outside, and the place seemed to be very busy- it was filled with men...

As we pulled up, Hallelujah said "Wait here, I need to go and have a word with the owner" and with that, he disappeared into the building. He emerged about five minutes later. As he opened my door, he bent down and quietly said "John, this is a Taliban restaurant. These men that you see are all Taliban. I have asked if we can sit and eat our food in the Women Only room!" He said it, again, so matter-of-factly!

I looked at the Lord as I walked through the crowded Taliban restaurant. They looked at me but they didn't see me! We went into the "Women Only" room and sat down. We had a lovely meal. We talked and laughed. We were all very relaxed! It was amazing! Then when we were finished, my two bodyguards went out to get the car ready. Then after five minutes, Hallelujah and I walked out, again, through a busy, Taliban filled restaurant, out to the waiting car! As I walked out, I was secretly taking pictures with my phone's camera, whilst saying to myself "No one will believe me!" I climbed into the awaiting car and then we raced off down the motorway!

I was amazed by what had happened! The Lord was showing Me His power in a new way that I had never experienced before. These men would have killed me at the drop of a hat! They were looking straight at me, but it was as if they couldn't see me. I could feel the Lord's protection around my heart. He was not letting any fear rise up in me, even though I could feel that there was fear and panic inside of me, wanting to break out, but I was very much aware of the Lord's power keeping my heart in a state of peace. The scripture became alive:

"Thou preparest a table before me in the presence of mine enemies." - Psalm 23:5a

Oh! He is so wonderful!

In Sahiwal we were blessed to be able to stay at a friend of Pastor Hallelujah's house. He was a very wealthy man, with a lot of influence in the local community. He lived on his own estate that was enclosed by an eight- foot wall. He had inherited it from his father, who was a Pastor before him. This man's name was Abraham and his wife's name was Sarah. Because of the situation in Pakistan, and because the local Police were concerned why this Englishman had come to Pakistan at this time to preach, as a precaution, Abraham had hired some armed Policemen to protect us whilst we were on his property.

As I was trying to get to sleep that night, every few minutes I would hear a whistle being blown for a few short seconds. This went on all night. In the morning, whilst at the breakfast table, being served porridge by my hostess, I asked Abraham what that noise was. "It is the bodyguards" he said" They have to blow a whistle in order to give a proper warning to anyone who would try to climb over the wall who would want to come and kill you. So that, if they shoot them dead, then they will face no prosecution because they have given them fair warning!" "Great!" I thought "maybe I shouldn't have asked..."

The time came for the first meeting. We had to wait on Abraham's estate until the police escort arrived, which should have been sent by the meetings organiser. We waited...and waited...No police showed up. A couple of the local Pastors had joined us and so, after talking to Hallelujah, they knew where we had to go and so we set off, hoping that the police were waiting for us at the meeting.

When we pulled up at the venue, Pastor Hallelujah said in disbelief "Oh, my God! It's in the streets!" The organisers had set up the meeting in the middle of the street in this Muslim area! instead of inside a secure building, or structure that could be defended if it needed be...Also, there was no police or security anywhere to be seen! I took a deep breath. "Okay Lord, let Thy will be done" I prayed silently under my breath as we entered into the meeting. It was very similar to the secret meeting back in Jarranwalla- a sea of beautiful colour, a mass of people dancing and swaying to the music. Beautiful curtains decked the platform, glaring lights and a loud rhythm being beaten out on some drums.

The Lord's presence was there, and that was all that I needed! I felt safe and secure. His boldness came upon me as I started to preach. At the end of the preaching I challenged the Muslims who were there to repent and put their faith in Jesus. About a third of the people there gave their lives to Him. Then I prayed for the sick, and the sick were healed! To finish off, I got them all to close their eyes and bow their heads, and as they did, Hallelujah and I, along with the other Pastors left the meeting as quickly and as quietly as we could!

On the way back to Abraham's house, there was much talk amongst the three Pastors. They didn't seem very happy. I knew that Pastor Hallelujah was concerned for my safety. The Lord had showed us His wonderful grace once again.

The next day I went to visit The Tabitha Sewing School that we had set up some four years before. This time the police escort did show up! It was a privilege to be able to meet these wonderful Christian sisters, who had faced rape and abuse at the hands of their Muslim employers, when they had worked as servants in their houses. In Pakistan, it is very hard for a Christian to find work. In a country that is ninety-eight percent Muslim, Christians are treated as second-class citizens. The sisters were very happy to meet us and we gave them each a gift from England. They proudly showed us the garments that they had made, and the Pastor who runs the School had told us of various testimonies of how the young ladies lives had changed because of being able to earn their own money with their own sewing businesses that they had set up after they had graduated from the school. I left feeling very humbled by these people but also, overwhelmed with joy at what the Lord was doing among them. He is doing a great work there and it is a privilege to be part of it.

The next meeting was to be held about a one hour drive out into the dark countryside. As we drove through the darkness, I thought about the meeting from the previous night. The Lord had protected us and had poured out His power again. I was very excited and was looking forward to the meeting, to see what the Lord would do. Again, we were joined by the same two Pastors from the previous meeting. They both claimed to have enjoyed themselves and so they were coming along to hear some more preaching by the foolish English boy!

As we pulled off of the main road, I noticed that the road we were driving along was filled with large pot-holes, so that you could only drive along this road at a very slow speed, in order to navigate around the holes and avoid any damage to the car. We drove for about another hour.

We knew that we were close to the venue because we had to drive around some water-buffalos that were laid down in the road, flatly refusing to move. The signs of civilization appeared. A few small buildings here and there. More cattle. Eventually we stopped. We were in the middle of nowhere! It was a small farming community. But they were a community of radical Muslims! The Pastor told me that they had been trying to plant a church here for some time, but every time that they had held a crusade, only a few of the villagers had come. When they had heard that a white man was preaching- the whole village had turned up to see! The Pastor had told me that one wrong word, and we may not make it out alive!

Great...

We waited inside a dark barn, sipping some tea. They were still busy organizing the people and the equipment. I noticed that one man who had joined us when we had arrived, was looking at me. Actually, he was staring at me, and I could discern in his eyes a spirit of murder. It wasn't a very pleasant look that he was giving me! I had seen that look many times before...

When it was time to start, we had to walk along the side of the curtains that formed the side walls of the meeting. Because it was set up in a narrow dusty track, there was not much room between the edge of the curtains and the local sewage gulley that ran along side the tent. "Lord, please don't let my feet slip!" I prayed as I inched along the narrow ledge to the front of the tent.

As I sat at the front, again, I noticed that there was no security! The Lord was stretching my faith all of the time that I was in Pakistan.

The meeting began with the various introductions that seemed to take up most of the time. Then one of the organizers spoke to Hallelujah, who then leaned over to me and quietly said "They have given you fifteen minutes to preach!" "WHAT!" I said, "All this way to preach for fifteen minutes- I don't think so!" The Holy Spirit didn't seem so pleased either! I said to Pastor Hallelujah, who was going to translate for me, "I'll preach as long as the Lord wants me to preach!" to which he smiled and nodded.

The Lord poured out His power, and His presence was wonderful. Again, at the end, I challenged them to repent and to give their lives to Jesus. About half of the people responded. Then I asked anyone who had any pain to stand up, and to place their hand upon their pain, where ever it was. Most of the people stood up. I prayed for the Lord to heal them, and then said "If you know that you have been healed, I want you wave your hands in the air!" Pastor Hallelujah translated it, and then there was a sea of hands waving in the air accompanied by a sea of huge smiles! They had not been smiling before this. Pastor Hallelujah turned and looked at me "They all got healed!" he said, with his usual matter-of-fact tone in his voice. I was over the moon!

We all climbed back into the car and set off along the very bumpy road, at a snail's pace. I noticed that everyone, including Hallelujah, seemed to be very quiet- almost nervous...

When we reached the main road, Pastor Hallelujah breathed a huge sigh of relief "Praise God, we made it out alive!" he said. I didn't really take much notice of what he said until we arrived back at Abraham's house.

When we all climbed out of the car, one of the local Pastors suddenly said "It's by God's grace that we are all still alive!" I was shocked at hearing these words! I knew that there was danger at the meeting, but it didn't seem too bad to me until they started to explain to Abraham where we had been and where the meeting had been held...

Abraham was shocked- he said to me "Where you were tonight is one of the most dangerous places around this area. It is a notoriously dangerous place. I wouldn't even drive there with a police escort!" "Why not?" I asked. "Well, the reason why the road to that area is so bumpy is because they dig it up deliberately, so that you have to drive slowly down it, so that they can shoot you and rob you. They will shoot you dead just to steal your mobile phone!" He said.

He shook his head "I can't believe that they organized a meeting for you there- one word from any one of those villagers, if they didn't like what you said, or even if they took offense because you are a white European and they would have killed you without any hesitation!" I looked around at the faces of the other Pastors. I could see a look of relief and of also concern on their faces. We had another meeting scheduled for the next evening. They didn't look like they were too eager to go!

The next day Hallelujah came up to me and said "My dear brother, I am sorry to tell you this, but last night there was a plot to kidnap you. One of the Pastors was told this at the meeting last night..." Apparently, the man with the murder in his eyes, and his brother, had an intention to kidnap me to get money, but the Lord had kept me safe.

I wasn't happy that there had been no security again. As I thought on everything, the Lord spoke to me "Do not tempt the Lord Thy God. Do not test My grace..." He said. I knew that I had to cancel the meeting. It was a miracle that we were still alive, and I knew that it was purely by God's grace. I couldn't expect the Pastors to put their lives on the line again just for me, and so I called the organizers and cancelled the meeting.

So, the next day was filled with sight-seeing! Abraham took me to see the Chief of Police who, apparently, wanted to meet me. We sat and had tea in his office, and then he gave us a police escort to a Museum that Abraham wanted to show me. After that, Abraham took me to the school that his father had founded. I got to preach and pray for the precious children there.

It was soon time to head back to Lahore, to finish teaching the Bible Students. The plan was to take them to a local park and to evangelize the Muslims by handing out Gospel Tracts. Pastor Hallelujah told me to be ready to leave very quickly once we had given out the tracts, because, he said, "That's when the enemy will rise up and attack!" We were all assembled in the park, and as I prayed for the group a large storm broke from out of nowhere! A huge wind swept up the dust into our eyes and it started to pour down with rain. We all took shelter under a canopy and decided that, maybe that it was the Lord that was stopping us, for some reason, that He, in His wisdom, only knew. We had a wonderful picnic together and enjoyed a wonderful time of fellowship.

The time in Pakistan was over. It was time to head to the airport and fly back to England. As I sat on the plane, I reflected upon all that had happened. All of the miracles that I had witnessed first- hand! The Lord had shown me His power to save, heal and deliver. I had received some feed-back from the Pastor that had organized the meetings- Muslims and Hindus had come to salvation and, along with Christians, had been healed and set free from various demonic influences. One Hindu boy, who was blind had received his sight! A Muslim family who had been oppressed by demonic forces had said that they had been set free! One man who was addicted to drugs had been delivered. Another woman who had severe pain when she walked had been totally healed. Even, some Jehovah Witnesses had been converted!

It had been the most dangerous time to go to Pakistan and yet, even though at times we had no protection from men, the Lord had kept us alive against all of the odds. The Lord had manifested His power and presence in such a tangible way. I had a huge sense of satisfaction-I had seen the Lord move in such mighty ways. He had shown me His power, as He had promised, if I would go where He would send me.

This time, I did not pray "Lord, please never ask me to go back to Pakistan" as I did on my first visit. No. The Lord had shown me that my life is in His hands, and that no one can take it from me apart from the Lord's will. No, I left Pakistan wondering "What's next?"

CHAPTER 8 ~ A BAD CASE OF LARYNGITIS

"Many are the afflictions of the righteous: but the Lord delivereth him out of them all." - Psalm 34:19

I'd had a sore throat hundreds of times over the last 12 years of preaching on the streets, it was no big deal! Well, that's what I thought…But this time I couldn't shake it, no matter what I did, my voice seemed to get more hoarse day by day.

"I've probably strained my vocal chords" or "It might be laryngitis?" were the excuses that I told myself, over and over, as the growing concern took up more of my thoughts each day. People began to comment and suggest that I go and see the doctor. "See the doctor over a petty sore throat?" I thought. I hadn't been to the doctors for years, and certainly not for something as insignificant as a sore throat.

Then, one day whilst driving home from work, the Holy Spirit spoke, just as I was passing A &E in Swindon, "Go and see someone about your throat!" He said, "Yeah, maybe I'll go tomorrow..." was my reply, knowing that I had no intention to. The following week, the Lord spoke again, just as I was passing A&E "Go and see someone about your throat!" His voice was calm but authorative, "Oh, yeah! I better had do something…." said I, knowing that I wasn't going to do anything. You know, you can only get away with so much with the Lord until He makes sure you get the message. "Go and see someone now!" His voice was clear. He was not happy.

I went.

The doctor was very nice, asking all sorts of questions about my lifestyle. I told him that it had been about nine months that I'd had a problem with my voice, to which he recommended that I go and see a specialist at the hospital. "oh, great! More waiting around in waiting rooms, wasting time!" thought I, "It's only laryngitis…"

The letter from the hospital dropped through my door about two weeks later. My appointment was in a weeks' time. "wow! That's quick! Usually you have to wait for ages before you get to see a specialist" were the nervous words that drifted through my mind..." It's only laryngitis!"

"Is it ok if I take a look?" said the throat Doctor, whilst pulling out of a drawer a rather long, black, flexible lead with a camera on the end." What are you going to do with that?" I asked, already knowing the answer.... Up the nose and down the back of the throat it went- not nice at all! After a few minutes of wiggling this way and that, he gently pulled it out. "Well Mr Dunn, I'm going to recommend you to see a specialist!" "I thought that you were the specialist...." Was the thought in my head, quickly followed by "I don't believe it! This is going to take forever! "But, as before, the appointment came through with an uneasy sense of urgency about it.

So a week later it was "Return of the throat Doctor, the sequel!" "Can I have a look?" was the anticipated question. That, I knew, would bring out the black, snake like probe, up the nose, down the throat- great! The doctor sat back in his chair and looked at me with a poker face, " I think it would be best to do a biopsy, as I can see that there is a suspicious lump on your vocal chords."

This was starting to become more than just laryngitis! So, again, a few weeks later, another invitation to the hospital made its way to my house. This involved being put to sleep, which hadn't happened to me since I was eleven, when I had a minor operation on my ears. I felt very apprehensive about it all, to say the least...

I arrived at the hospital in plenty of time. One of my things is to be on time, or early but never late! A nurse showed me to the changing room, which looked more like a Janitors cupboard than a changing room, being filled with lockers, buckets and mops. After I had put on the famous hospital gown (that is specially designed never to do up at the back, and made with very slippery material, so that it always slips off of your shoulders) the nurse put on me some special socks to prevent any blood clots forming in my legs. The dressing gown that I bought was the one that I always wore at home. When I say "always", I mean, always! in the hospital environment it absolutely stank of my two dogs, Barnie and Betsie. I apologised to the nurse about the smell, but she was fine about it, being a dog lover herself.

"Ok, a small, sharp scratch...!" (an expression that I was going to hear many times over the coming few months) said the nurse in the operating theatre, as she inserted the canular into the back of my hand. That was the last thing I remembered, then, suddenly, I was waking up, with the

Throat Doctor talking to me with a very concerned look on his face (Why do they speak to you as soon as you wake up? You have no idea what they're saying to you, it's enough to try a figure out where on earth you are!)

I went home in a bit of a daze, probably due to the anaesthetic, and partly due to the look that I saw on the Throat Doctor's face. "Now the long wait for the biopsy results..." I thought to myself. Even though it was only two weeks before the results were ready, it seemed like two months! (they came two days after my fiftieth birthday!) I found myself back at the hospital, nervously waiting in the Waiting Room. I decided to pass the time by scrolling through Facebook on my phone, when, suddenly, a verse appeared on the screen that The Lord had been highlighting to me as I read the Bible in my personal time with The Lord.

"Many are the afflictions of the righteous: but the Lord delivereth him out of them all." (Psalm 34:19)

Suddenly the Holy Spirit spoke..." Look up the meaning of the word "AFFLICTIONS" He said. On my Bible app, I quickly found the word- "Ra" in the Greek, which, as I read the meaning of the word, only one word stood out .... "MALIGNANT!" I knew that The Lord, in His mercy, was preparing me for some news that I wouldn't want to hear...

I was called into the throat Doctor's office. He sat there, with his poker face on, and some sheets of paper laid on the desk in front of him. "Please, take a seat Mr Dunn," he said in that voice that doctors use when they want to try to calm you, just about when they're going to deliver some news that's going to tear apart your entire world!

"The results of the biopsy do not indicate cancer" he said " Yes! Just as I thought!" were the words in my head that were rudely interrupted by his next sentence... "But I say that it is cancer!" That kind of rained on my parade! as they say! " I'm going to recommend you to see a specialist," he said, " but I thought that you were the specialist!"   (would I ever get to meet this elusive specialist, I thought?) "I'm transferring you to Oxford, they have much more of a specialist team there" were the last words that I heard from the throat Doctor in Swindon.

So now it was a case of driving all the way to Oxford, which was about an hour's drive from Swindon, not knowing whether it was cancer or not! I was hoping that the results of the biopsy would trump the throat Doctor's professional opinion.

From Bad to Worse

I sat in front of three, poker-faced specialists. One of them pulled out my file, with the results from an emergency CT and MRI scan that I'd had done the previous week. The throat Specialist spoke "The results from the scan indicate a swelling in your vocal chords..'''" mate, I could have told you that," thought I! "The MRI scan has also picked up an abnormality in your liver, which we will have to investigate." "WHAT! Now there's a problem with my liver! This is too much!" I was already beginning to decide in my mind that I would not be returning for any more appointments.

"We agree with the Swindon throat Doctor's diagnosis" said the specialist." But you haven't even looked down my ...." "Is it ok if I take a look?" he said. My heart sank, "yes!" I replied, waiting for the black snake to appear, and sure enough, up the nose, down the back of the throat it went.

Satisfied with what he saw, I was sent away with the prospect of facing another biopsy. I left the hospital, vowing to myself that there was no way that I was going to return! But time would soon tell another story...

It was after attending a Bible study with Paul and Merle that the cancer in my throat started to manifest itself in a huge lump on the front part of my throat. It grew to the size of an avocado within a few days, and the pain was immense! I had no choice but to call for the paramedics at one o'clock in the morning, so that I could get some relief from the fire that was raging in my throat.

After going to the local medical centre and chatting to the Doctor about Jesus, I arrived home and the lump on my throat suddenly burst, with a foul-smelling pus oozing out of it! But all the pain had suddenly gone! For the first time in a year I was without pain! Even my voice sounded clearer and stronger than it had done for a long time. "Wow!" I thought, "I am healed! It wasn't cancer after all but a boil or some kind of cyst!" I reasoned with myself.

In the meantime, I had agreed to go to the hospital for the second biopsy, just to prove that the results of the first biopsy was the truth and not the opinion of the throat Doctors that were saying that it was cancer.

It was a Tuesday when my wife dropped me off at The Churchill Hospital in Oxford, for the routine biopsy. I was expecting to be in and out within a few hours, just like before, little did I know that my whole life was about to change forever...

"Would you like to follow me, please, Mr. Dunn?" the nurse asked as she led the way to the operating theatre. I tagged along behind her, all the while trying not to let the hospital gown reveal my hind quarters to any passer-by. "Ok, a small, sharp scratch!" the Nurse said. "Of course, my dear! it always is..." I thought to myself. "Lord, let your will be done!" were the words that saw me off to sleep.

Then I Awoke....

Again, I was confronted with the face of a very concerned Throat Specialist. I immediately noticed something to be very wrong, due to the fact that a large tube was coming out from the front of my throat. As the Specialist spoke, the words "went terribly wrong!" and "narrow windpipe" "stop you from strangling to death!" were the only words that I caught hold of. I couldn't fully grasp what was going on, my mind was hazy with the effects of the anaesthetic, but I knew something terrible had happened.

They whisked me away on my hospital bed, down corridors, people coming and going, overhead lights, signs, talking, and that distinct hospital smell...soon we arrived at the Blenheim Head and Neck Ward. I remember waking up in the late hours of the night to silence, except for the occasional "beeps" from the hospital machines, only to see my faithful wife sat next to my bed. I wanted to speak to her, to reassure her, to ask her what had happened to me, but I couldn't speak, due to tube that was in my throat I didn't realise at that point that I wouldn't be able to speak naturally ever again!...

Apparently, because of the avocado lump that had come up and burst on my throat, it had caused the inside of my windpipe to narrow due to the swelling and so when the Doctor had come to do the Panendoscopy (the examination of the upper trachea, larynx and oesophagus) and the biopsy (the removal of a sample of the lump on my vocal chords) he was concerned at the amount of blood loss and the swelling that had already occurred in my throat, so as a precautionary measure, he performed an emergency Tracheostomy (the insertion of a tube through the windpipe to ensure and protect the airway).

I didn't realise until later, but I was in shock from the trauma at what had happened. I had a strap around my neck, holding the tube in place, that felt like a dog collar. I felt completely helpless, I couldn't remove the tube and say, "Sorry! But I don't need this, I'm going home!" I couldn't even speak to the people around me, which was the most terrifying thing of all!

You see, when they do a Tracheostomy, your body starts to produce more secretions (mucus or phlem) to cope with it and protect the windpipe. The problem with that is, it blocks the tube in your throat when you cough, and thus, it cuts off your air! This kept happening to me. I would cough, and the phlem would block the tube, so that I couldn't breathe! But, I couldn't tell anyone what was happening, because I couldn't speak.

They had arranged for an MRI scan and an X-ray for me, to check that everything was ok. They wheeled me down the corridor in my bed, down to the place where they were to take these scans. All the while, I was coughing and almost drowning (that's how it felt!) and trying to make them know what was happening to me, but the nurse (whom I will call Heavy Handed, for so she was!) who was with me just kept saying " It's alright, just relax, just relax…"

Now, being a Christian, violence is forbidden, but I must confess that, if I could of, I think I would have punched Nurse Heavy Handed square in the face, purely out of fear and out of frustration! "I'm choking to death, and you keep telling me to relax!" I thought that I was going to die. I had nearly choked three times just on the way to the X-ray. I had never felt so vulnerable before, so much in danger of losing my life, even though I had been in situations when my life had been on the line for the Gospel, this was different. There was no glory to be gained by choking to death on a hospital bed whilst being told to "just relax!"

I spent the days just staring into space, thinking, wondering how my life would be from now on. The most painful thing was to realise that I would never preach the Gospel again! Never talk to someone about my precious Saviour, never argue with someone on the streets, never lift my voice to warn people of the coming wrath of God upon the children of disobedience! Oh! the most blessed thing for me had been snatched away! it felt like the rug had truly been pulled out from under my feet.

Who was I to be from now on? What was I to do? In the midst of all the confusion, all the heart- searching and sorrow, my Lord's peace remained like an anchor in my heart. I didn't go down the "why me?" road for very long, knowing that it would only lead to a dead end. After about four days of being battered by all sorts of fears and woes, sorrows and pains, the Light of my Saviour's love started to break through all of the darkness that had surrounded me. He was with me still, reassuring me and calming the storm that had raged in my heart and mind. His tender presence caused the shock and the trauma to melt away and to give way to His peace and serenity.

I smiled for the first time.

Gradually, the sun was coming out again and the rain clouds had vanished over the horizon of hope! Oh, lovely Jesus! How people miss out when they confuse Jesus with a religion. The reality of His power was changing my heart, taking out the sting of death and replacing it with the balm of life!

The nurses noticed the change. I started to co-operate with them. They had a job to do, to get me adjusted to caring for myself, to be able to deal with living with this tube in my throat- how to change it, which, at first, seemed a task impossible for me to do, to draw out a four-inch tube from your own throat, wash it, and replace it into the hole, gaping at you in the mirror! But the Lord was with me, and working in me. I knew I could do it, and that everything was going to be ok.

Soon visitors came and started to try and lift me the best they knew how. Peter and Karen were the first to come, but I still wasn't in a right place to receive visitors, even though I was desperate for company! It was lovely to have people come and break up the long days of just sitting.

A group of brothers came from The Vine Church in Swindon. We had a wonderful time of prayer and open worship, much to the amusement of the other patients on the ward. The next day, I was moved by the hospital staff into a room by myself! It had an en-suite, which was a real winner! "Thank you, Lord! For your favour and blessings," I thought.

Many people had prayed and were praying for God to heal me miraculously. I had resigned the results to the Lord's wisdom- I trusted Him. He knew what to do for the best. In this situation, all I knew was that He had a plan greater than I could imagine. It was, and always is, a case of resting in the trust that comes from knowing Him.

He is good all of the time.

The Lord continued to pour out His grace and presence upon me. I went from being sullen to being filled with joy. When I say filled with joy, I was overflowing with joy! So much so, that I had to go into the bathroom, lock the door, and dance around the room, in order to release this joy, which was so overpowering, that it felt that if I didn't release it, I would simply burst! I knew that The Lord had His hand on me- the circumstances were nothing to get excited about, yet, I was having a continued feast of joy and happiness!

Yes, dancing with joy around a bathroom whilst having cancer and never being able to speak again…

It wasn't long before I was to be released back home, but not before all of the specialists got together for a meeting to discuss the next step. Again, I found myself surrounded by poker-faced medical professionals, each with their own part to play in my recovery. "The results from the biopsy show that it is definitely cancer" said the throat Specialist, who then proceeded to unfold the master plan… it was a choice between a full laryngectomy or not to continue with the treatment, go home, and basically, die! Not much of a choice, really!

Now, a laryngectomy is when they remove the whole of your larynx, your vocal chords, rendering you speechless. But because of the avocado that grew and burst on my throat, leaving a rather nasty wound, they had a plastic surgeon come and look at what he could do to repair all the damage that had been done by the cancer. He proposed a procedure which basically involved the cutting of a large section of the skin and flesh on the left shoulder, rotating it over onto the throat, stitching it on and then closing up the wound on the shoulder by pulling both sides of the cut together and stitching it up, making the left clavicle and shoulder area extremely tight. He would also have to divert an artery in my mouth down to my throat.

Now when I had been on the ward, I had seen some guys come in who had had a basic laryngectomy, and, boy! did they look ill afterwards! I remember looking at the awful scar that went from the ear down to the throat and thinking how ugly it looked. Little did I know, but I was in for a whole lot worse…….

It was lovely to be home! The familiar smells, the comfort, not having to be injected every night in the stomach, and, not having someone appear at your bedside first thing in the morning to take blood, was a real blessing! I had a brother from Germany contact me. He had it in his heart to come and pray for me.

So, after a few days, our dear German brother arrived at our house. I had travelled with this man in the past, and I found him to be one of the most genuine Christians that I have ever met.

Now, since this trouble all began, I had been doing everything I knew how to try and defeat this cancer. I had prayed, fasted, spoken out the Word of God and confessed it over my life. I'd had people pray for me from all around the world, America, Pakistan, Israel, many people were praying for me.

I'd had deliverance prayer from a sister in America, I'd changed my diet to a vegan diet (even though it was for only three weeks!) And now, my German brother was going to pray for me and do deliverance prayer, which involves breaking any curses and casting out any demons that might be working. I was hoping and praying that, when I had to go back into hospital for the laryngectomy, that they would examine me and find that there was no more cancer, and that I had been completely healed!

It didn't go that way…

The day came when I had to go back to the hospital. I knew what I was in for. It had to be done, there was no way around it. I had prayed for courage and the Lord, in His mercy, gave to me His peace in my heart and mind. It is truly amazing, how the Lord can protect you from fear, and worry if you will put your trust in Him.

A New Beginning

It was July 4th 2017 and I was put into room 14 on the head and neck ward. The night before the operation, I had a visit from the Throat Specialist, the Plastic Man and the Anaesthetist. All of them wanting to go through what was going to happen the following day. I already knew what was coming. I was trying not to think about it, but it seemed like everyone wanted to make sure I had the picture – I did. And it didn't look pretty! I spent some time in prayer and also, contemplating what life was going to be like without the ability to speak. I resolved myself to just take it as it comes, climb the mountains, cross the bridges, etc, when I got to them…

I still wrestled with the thought of not being able to preach! not being able to teach the Bible in the Bible study that I had been leading for the past nine years and most of all, not being able to tell people about Jesus. Not being able to speak- it was going to be a whole new way of life, but I knew that, in all of it, the Lord had a plan...

"Ok, a small, sharp scratch...!" The familiar phrase that started the next stage in the fight against cancer. I was hoping that whilst I was asleep that I would have another spiritual experience, like the one I had as a young boy, all those years ago, whilst on the Dentists' chair, but before I knew what was happening, I was waking up in Intensive Care.

Again, just like the two previous times, I woke up to a big shock! I cannot put it into words, the first time that I saw myself in the mirror. I looked like Frankenstein. My neck looked horrific. The stitches seemed to run all over my throat forming a kind of jigsaw puzzle appearance. They looked like huge worms wrapped around my neck.

I had a cut that went from just beneath my right ear, down my neck, along the front of my throat, up the left side of my neck, then along my left collarbone, over my left shoulder, finishing about half way down it. My neck looked deflated, from where they had cut away the larynx some surrounding tissue and my mouth was all twisted from where the Plastic Man had re-routed an artery from inside my mouth, down towards the hole on the front of my throat. Most of my neck, my left shoulder and chest region, and my mouth were numb. I had a large wound on my left shoulder from the cut of the skin and flesh graft.

I had been in surgery for thirteen hours!

It was major surgery.

I was in major shock.

Again, as before, when I awoke, there beside me was my darling wife! The sight of Rachel sat next to the bed brought me great comfort. I could tell by the look on her face, her eyes being wide and round, that she found it hard to see me like that, but I also knew that Rachel would be a rock and would deal with it without showing any fuss.

It wasn't long before I was being transported up to The Blenheim Head and Neck Ward. It was late. It was dark and very quiet on the ward. It wasn't long before I had drifted off to sleep. I was put in a bed that was closest to the Nurse Station, so that, if anything went wrong, they could get to me quickly. Opposite me was a huge, fat man, who was married to a little Filipino woman, who seemed to take exceptional care of him. All day and all night, this man played some kind of Monastic chanting music that was almost hypnotic – it was horrible!

On top of that, I had a body full of anaesthetic, which played havoc with my mind. I had seen my father, after he had an operation when he had cancer, come out of the operation, and his mind was never quite the same again. I was praying that wouldn't be the case with me...

The nights were terrifying. As I would drift off to sleep, my mind would be filled with people shouting all kinds of blasphemies, to which, in my mind, I would rebuke and disagree with. I started to hallucinate, seeing all kinds of creatures, birds, ants, fish swimming past me on the floor. I just sat there watching them. Strange shapes and objects would appear in front of my eyes, buzzing and spinning. I could almost reach out and touch them. I knew that my mind was under attack and I was afraid that I might not regain it! I asked Rachel to pray for my sanity.

Usually the anesthetic wears off after a few days, but even after a week, I still couldn't walk properly and the nights were getting worse! I had only managed to get two hours sleep per night, since the first visit to hospital which was a month ago. It added to the torment. I knew that I was in danger of losing my mind. I would cry out to God from inside my head, begging Him to protect my mind, and restore me to sanity again. I think that this was the scariest thing that I had encountered so far, knowing that I was not in my right mind, with no guarantee that it would change! Such torture, but nobody could see it and I couldn't tell anybody about it. But, praise God, my Lord heard me, and delivered me from all of my fears, restoring my mind to His peace and stability.

Soon people started to visit me. My eldest sister, Jill, to whom I am close to, when she first saw me, burst into tears and ran out of the ward because the sight of my neck was a bit too much for her. Other visitors were visibly shaken as well. A few of them commented "Wow! They've really cut you up!" But it wasn't too long before things started to improve.

The Lord started to fill me with His familiar joy, to which, all I could do was to praise Him for His love and faithfulness towards me. Soon all the drains that they had fitted to drain off the blood, were removed. The catheter was removed, and boy! that was an experience! The nurse said "ok, take a deep breath..." "I wonder why?" thought I! Then she pulled the end of the catheter out- to say it brought tears to my eyes is an understatement!

I had the opportunity on many occasions to experience what a woman feels when she waxes her legs (I can't believe that they do it voluntary!).

They had put a canular into the artery on the inside of my leg, right next to my groin, so the plasters were stuck to the hair on my leg, just below the hip joint. Now nurses are generally gentle creatures, but it seems to be that when they have an opportunity to rip off a plaster and take a large portion of the hair with it, they take no prisoners! And my nurses were no exception!

They soon had taken me off the drips, and I was able to start eating and drinking again -once I had passed the swallow test! (This involved drinking water dyed blue, whilst being X-rayed, to see if there were any leaks from the food pipe into the surrounding neck. If there was, that meant more surgery!)

Praise God, all went well, I passed. The food that I could eat had to be pureed so that it was easier to take in. After a few days, the speech therapist came to show me how to clean the speech valve that was in my throat (it involved sticking a long, thin brush into the valve in my throat with the aid of a mirror and a torch) Not a very glamorous procedure, but a necessary one.

One day as I was sat in the bed, the presence of the Lord had been with me all morning. I suddenly became aware that there were two hands placed on my neck, with the thumbs stroking me just beneath my chin. There was no one behind me, or beside me, but there was definitely someone caressing my neck! This lasted for a few minutes. It was the Lord. I knew that He was showing me that He was the one who was healing my neck, and that He was right there with me.

Oh! Lovely Jesus! Truly, He is the Good Shepherd that takes care of His sheep.

At last, the day came that I was to be set free, once again. I was a bit nervous with the idea of going home, away from all the people who had worked so hard to help me recover, away from the safety of knowing that there were people around me if I suddenly needed them...But, once again, my Lord's presence was reassuring and I knew that I was safe in His hands. Even in the hospital, the Lord had surrounded me with nurses who were believers, so that they were able to encourage me and pray for me.

After this kind of operation, according to the Doctors, it takes a minimum of about seven months to be able to eat normal food again and a normal diet.

I was eating a normal diet after three weeks!

I had to have a course of Radiotherapy, every day for six weeks. This was the completion of my treatment. They told me about the side effects of the treatment, of which there was quite a few. Every time that I would be led on the table, ready to have the treatment, I would pray Psalms 23 and 91, which are psalms of protection. Every week I would have regular check-ups by the doctors and nurses to help me deal with the side effects. This is how a typical conversation would go…

Nurse: "Any problems with drinking?"

Me: "No!"

Nurse: "Any problems with eating?"

Me: "No!"

Nurse: "What are you taking for your pain?"

Me: "I have no pain!"

Nurse: "Any sore skin?"

Me: "No!"

Nurse (laughing!) "Are you sure that you're having your treatment?"

I suffered no side effects, apart from some skin on my throat turned red!

Again, I could see the Lord's protection and care for me. He is so faithful. He brought me through the darkest hour of my life by His grace. He lavished upon me His presence and love. Through it, He has brought me closer to Himself and for that I am eternally grateful! I can repeat what my dear father had said to me eight years previously, "This cancer has been a blessing to me!"

EPILOGUE

"But what things were gain to me, those I counted loss for Christ. Yea doubtless, and I count all things but loss for the excellency of the knowledge of Christ Jesus my Lord: for Whom I have suffered the loss of all things, and do count them but dung, that I may win Christ." (Philippians 3:7-8)

My friend, I pray that, by reading this book, that your eyes might have been opened to the fact that God is real and that you can know Him! I mean, really know Him! That He is the Living God, and that we can know Him through a personal relationship with His Son, Jesus Christ. I hope that you have realized that this book is not about John Dunn but about the One who has done great things in my life.

Since the day that I met the Lord, my life has forever been changed. He took a hold of a foolish boy and He has shown me great and marvellous things! I have cast out demons from people, laid hands on the sick and seen them healed, performed "Exorcisms" upon peoples' houses, seen both angels and demons, preached the Gospel at both funerals and weddings, made a film, made television programmes, been interviewed by journalists, appeared on television, been in the news, spoken to Government Officials about Christ and travelled the world and I have preached the Gospel to thousands of people!

There are so many things that I have had to leave out of this book. So many healings on the streets, so many miracles wrought in the lives of people that we've met. I simply couldn't write them all down! And none of it is because of me! It has all been by His grace and by His grace alone! It is all for His glory and that His Name might be magnified in all the earth!

He has led me through the valley of the shadow of death, only to emerge the other side with a greater knowledge and understanding of who He is!

He been so faithful to me and to my family. People may ask, because He is a healing God, that why didn't He heal me of cancer? He did! but He did it according to His infinite wisdom, which was for my profit. It has been and is a blessing to me.

Trust is not about having all of the answers or knowing everything that is happening or that will happen to you in your life. To trust God is to put everything into His hands, and then KNOW that all things that come are sent for your good because He is good and He is in control. I love Him and therefore I trust Him, no matter what...

I have been rejected by many people. I have been despised and hated by many. I have had so many lies and slanderous accusations spoken against me. I have been ridiculed by believers as well as unbelievers. I have been threatened so many times with violence. I have had people who have tried to kill me for preaching.

I have been in trouble with the police more times than I could mention. I've spent a lot of time away from my wife and from my children. Like I have mentioned in these pages, I've been spat at, shouted at, pushed, shoved, punched, had so many different things either thrown over me or at me. I've had sickness and disease. I've preached in the rain, snow, frost, hail, wind and blistering heat. I've had no money, and I've had plenty. But like the great Apostle Paul, I can say that;

"...I have learned, in whatsoever state I am, therewith to be content." (Philippians 4:11)

I am satisfied in the Lord. He is enough.

Can you truly say that you are completely satisfied, dear reader?

To all of my dear brothers and sisters who know me in the Lord, I thank the Lord for having met you, and for the love that He has given to me for you. I haven't been able to mention everybody in this book, but I carry you always in my heart.

And if you have read this book, and you do not know the Lord, then my prayer for you is that you would begin on this great journey of faith and discovery of the Great and Mighty God and Father of our Lord Jesus Christ.

That you might discover His love for you.

He is worth more than life itself!

As for me... I am continuing on with my Lord and Master to new and greater pastures.

I am still teaching the Bible, teaching up to six hours in one session.

You have just read the fruit of a new labour for me! maybe more books will follow, if the Lord wills…

I CANNOT BE STOPPED, EITHER BY MAN OR DEMON!

I HAVE SET MY FOREHEAD AS FLINT

And will continue on until that day when He calls for me to lay down my sword, to cross over the river Jordan and into the Promised Land and to enter in through the gates into His Heavenly City.

Until then…

Grace and peace to you all in the mighty Name of Jesus Christ.

Amen.

~ John Dunn

A FINAL WORD TO THE READER

My friends, if after reading this book, you feel that you would like to enter into a relationship with God and begin a new life but are not quite sure on how to take that next step, or if after reading this book you have some questions regarding faith or the things written within these

pages, or even if you feel that you have been blessed by this book and would like to send a word of encouragement to me, then here is my email address by which you can contact me:

johndunn333000@yahoo.co.uk

Grace and Peace to you all in Jesus' mighty Name.

Printed in Poland
by Amazon Fulfillment
Poland Sp. z o.o., Wrocław